Praise for Dave Mason and *Only You Know & I Know*

"It's an honor to be asked to reflect on my dear longtime friend Dave Mason. Our separate musical journeys started in our mother country, England, back in those early days of Traffic and more. David came from royal creative roots, and my fellow players and I were in awe! As you read the long-lasting musical journey described in this book you will be reminded of the huge influence Dave Mason has had as a trailblazer. And it will also be a reminder that, to this day, his musical integrity shines brightly for us all to see."

– Mick Fleetwood

"I discovered Dave Mason by listening to Traffic, one of the greatest supergroups of all time. Their first and second albums should be in anybody's top 100. Dave's songwriting, guitar work, and vocals are easily recognized in their music, and his artistry lives on today in the studio and on his never-ending rock tour. Want to get some juicy rock history? Read this book!"

– Alice Cooper

"It was such a pleasure singing with David, a great songwriter and a great friend."

– Graham Nash

"I sometimes judge a song's greatness by how many times I've actually played that song myself. I've probably played 'Feelin' Alright?' hundreds of times in my life. Dave is not just a great songwriter, he's a great singer and a very underrated guitarist. I've had the pleasure of singing, playing, and hanging with Dave. He's always fun and inspiring!"

– Sammy Hagar

"Dave Mason is one of rock and roll's most talented and prolific composers. His songs were the centerpieces of more than a few timeless albums by such groups and artists as Traffic, Delaney & Bonnie, and Joe Cocker, not to mention his own iconic recordings!"

– Michael McDonald

"I think he has a fantastic touch. I love the way he plays guitar. And his songs are great."

– Eric Clapton

ONLY You KNOW & I Know

DAVE MASON

with Chris Epting

DTM
Entertainment

Editorial and project management by Scott B. Bomar for Fourth and State.
Book production by Adept Content Solutions.

Cover design by Patrick Crowley.
Cover photo by Lorrie Sullivan via Getty Images.
Back cover photo by Chris Jensen.

Lyrics and photographs reprinted with permission of the rights holders.
See Permissions page for additional details.

Library of Congress Cataloging-in-Publication Data available upon request.

Hardback ISBN: 9798218380175
Ebook ISBN: 9798218380182

DTM Entertainment
First printing
davemasonmusic.com

For Nora

Contents

Foreword

by coauthor Chris Epting

He was sitting in his home studio late one night, and I'm not even sure he was aware that I had wandered into the room and sat down on a couch behind him. From the speakers roared a wild and rollicking long-ago show. I believe it was from New Year's Eve at the Cow Palace in San Francisco, 1978. The Dave Mason Group was wrapping up a blistering version of "Only You Know and I Know." The lights were low, and I could see him smiling to himself. His guitar solo was fluid, expressive, and tasteful as ever. You could hear that everybody in that band was playing as if their lives depended on it. When he realized I was sitting behind him, he shook his head, chuckling, and said, "That was one hell of a group. Those guys were just amazing." That he left himself out the equation was not surprising to me at this point. As I had already learned over the course of a couple of years working on this book with him, Dave Mason is a lot of things, but he's not your typical legendary musician.

There are terms that I have developed in my head when I think about him. Reluctant rock star. Quiet giant. Laid-back legend and more. Maybe that's why he's not the household name like Clapton or Beck. I don't think that really matters to him. He knows who he is, and he knows what he's done. But he also never fails to give credit to that band from the 1970s. Or his current band for that matter. I think he's always been a guy who just basically wanted to be another player in the band. But it didn't quite work out that way because he's more than that. He's a remarkably gifted singer and songwriter in addition to being one of the most interesting and underrated guitar players of his generation. Dave has not managed to thrive and survive on the strength of massive hit records and a well-cultivated public image. Rather, it's been his no-nonsense, practical work ethic that seems to stem from his father. Put your nose to the grindstone and get it done. No excuses. No shying away from the work that is needed to support oneself. Wherever we have worked together on this book, from the beautiful shores of Maui to the crisp high-altitude in Nevada, his demeanor has always remained the same. Same sly, wry smile and subtle chuckle when he recounts the past. Same dismissive shrugging of the shoulders and eye rolling when you express to him how profound you think his influence has been on music. That's not to say that he can't be a handful. Stubborn, strong-willed, and fiercely independent in his thinking—I can understand why some bridges have been burned along the way. Yet, when he straps on the Stratocaster and begins to play and the notes cascade—be they tender, biting, sexy, joyful, or ethereal—fences are mended. All is forgiven. Until the next time.

Back in the 1970s, when so many of us teenagers were coming of age, carefully choosing which concerts we wanted to see based on our budgets, placing your money on Dave Mason was always a sure bet. We got lots of bang for the buck. You knew you were going to get an impeccably diverse set list that would touch upon Mason's time with Jimi Hendrix and Traffic, along with the deep dive into his own sparkling solo career. You would get a few free-form jams featuring some of the best players of the day. You would experience everything from cosmic, soaring rock and roll to down-home blues to expansive prog rock to timeless raise-the-roof anthems. And everything was made better by that resonant, deep, weirdly reassuring voice provided by Mr. Mason. It was a voice that sang to you in a way that made clear, "No matter what is happening in your life, no matter what you are going through right now, just relax and let the music carry you through. Everything's going to be alright."

He's had it all; he's lost it all. And that pattern has repeated many times in his life. Thankfully, he has entered a long chapter in life that is not only triumphant but healthy on all the levels that it needs to be. When I watch him and his wonderful wife, Winifred, going about their lives, it's easy to forget who he is: a playful old soul at peace with his place in the universe, musical and otherwise. But when you go through old boxes and photo albums—when you listen to the records and let your mind drift back to the power and force that he brought on stage for thousands upon thousands of nights—you realize that you truly are in the presence of someone who changed the game.

And when he sits in his studio night after night, retooling and trying to perfect new music that he's working on, you also recognize that he's not one to rest on his laurels. Because that's not what true artists do. They push forward, they reach for more, and they explore their innermost journeys. I think that's what I admire most about Dave Mason. For him, it's never about looking behind. Even getting him to consider writing a book was no small feat. In the end, I think the only reason he decided to do it was that he realized that by confronting and documenting his past, it would only help him focus more on the future.

I hope this book inspires you, the reader, to dig even deeper into the music, to fully realize and appreciate what this unassuming singer and guitar player has given us over all of these years. Why this man has not been nominated for the Rock & Roll Hall of Fame for his solo work is beyond me.

Road Dogs

Every night, every day, I let the music just take me away
Feels so good I can't let it go, I'll still be rockin' at the very last show
I can't stop, sure like to stay, but we keep rollin' down that old highway

We're road dogs, just wanna play
You got a problem, we'll rock it away
We're road dogs, we come to your town
We ain't foolin' when we lay it down
We're road dogs

On stage in the light, just makes me wanna play for you all night
Something old, something new, we're all just players in this rock and roll stew
We keep rollin' down this road, we kinda like it if the truth be told

We're road dogs, just wanna play
You got a problem, we'll rock it away
We're road dogs, we come to your town
We ain't foolin' when we lay it down
We're road dogs

Settle down, stay at home, but something tells me we're just born to roam

We're road dogs, just wanna play
You got a problem, we'll rock it away
We're road dogs, we come to your town
We ain't foolin' when we lay it down
We're road dogs

PREFACE

Road Dogs

I'm one of those fortunate few who has made a living following their passion. I can't read or write music, so I'm not exactly an "A" student in this field. And yet, I realize I've written some lasting songs that have touched people's hearts.

Songwriting has been my magic carpet that has allowed me to go places I otherwise never would have been. Along the way, I've met some of the most wonderful and interesting people—as well as some of the worst. I've been part of many intimate moments in people's lives— the back seat of a car, the bedroom, driving down a highway with no particular destination in mind. Couples have used my songs at their weddings. Then there was the Marine I met at a Toys for Tots concert in Atlanta who told me that he and a friend were stuck in a foxhole for three days in Vietnam and if it hadn't been for the Jimi Hendrix and Dave Mason tapes, "We would have gone crazy." It's an odd thing to be such a private part of other people's lives—their joys and heartaches, their loves and losses—and yet not know them by name.

I've performed and recorded with dozens of different artists: Paul McCartney, George Harrison, Michael Jackson, Stevie Wonder, Steve Winwood, The Spencer Davis Group, Carlos Santana, Eric Clapton, The Rolling Stones, Jimi Hendrix, Cass Elliot, Graham Nash, Fleetwood Mac, and Stephen Stills among them. My career has had great highs and tremendous lows. I've played to 30, and I've played to 300,000, and I've played everything in between. In 2004, I was inducted into the Rock & Roll Hall of Fame as a founding member of the group Traffic.

You might ask, how did it all start? And what happened along the way?

At the age of five, I spent fourteen months in the hospital repairing and recovering from a fall that developed into a rare childhood affliction called a Perthes hip. I've been married four times and divorced three. I've been bankrupt twice. I've outlived my son, gone through three earthquakes, and—two weeks after moving to St. Thomas—was hit by Hurricane Hugo. I've also overcome years of substance abuse and have definitely been overserved.

And I have survived the music business.

I'm a private person by nature, so the thought of writing a memoir sounded much too intrusive. Nevertheless, here it is.

I've tried not to be bitter. I've kept love alive, never stopped believing in myself, and never given up, no matter what obstacles I've had to overcome. I pay little attention to those who say, "It can't be done." As I sit here to recount my life, with so many highs and lows, I am glad I haven't left this good Earth yet because I don't want to be the guy who said, "I wish I had."

Only You Know and I Know

Only you know and I know
All the love that we've got to show
So don't refuse to believe it
By reading too many meanings

'Cause you know that I mean what I say
So don't go and ever take me the wrong way
You know you can't go on gettin' your own way
'Cause if you do, it's gonna get you someday

We're both here to be pleasin'
Oh, no, no, not deceivin'
But it's hard to believe it
When you've been so mistreated

'Cause you know that I mean what I say
So don't go and ever take me the wrong way
You know you can't go on gettin' your own way
'Cause if you do, it's gonna get you someday

If I seem to mislead you
It's just my craziness comin' through
But when it comes down to just two
I ain't no crazier than you

'Cause you know that I mean what I say
So don't go and ever take me the wrong way
You know you can't go on gettin' your own way
'Cause if you do, it's gonna get you someday

Only you know and I know
Only you know and I know
Only you know and I know
Only you know and I know

CHAPTER ONE

Only You Know and I Know

December 1968

I was driving to another band meeting at the home of Chris Blackwell, the manager of Traffic and the head of our label, Island Records. Blackwell lived with Josephine Heimann and her seven-year-old daughter, Francis—the child who delivered the spoken-word portion on "Hole in My Shoe," the first song I'd ever written and Traffic's biggest hit (#2 on the charts). I didn't know what the meeting was about. It had to be something good, though—maybe an upcoming American tour or something related to the release of our second album.

When we exploded on the scene just a year before, it was heavy stuff. Just a couple of years earlier, I had been out in the audience, crushed up near the stage staring up in awe at The Beatles and The Rolling Stones. Now they were out in the crowd watching Traffic, right alongside Eric Clapton, Jimi Hendrix, and many other luminaries. Hell, I was now in the studio actually *working* with these guys, all because of how intrigued and entranced everyone was with Traffic.

Being a member of Traffic was the ultimate musical calling card. The normally cynical music press was genuinely interested in our band, as it was Steve Winwood's first project after leaving the Spencer Davis Group. Given Winwood's fame, expectations were exceedingly high.

I had become the surprise of the band, no matter that I'd already sung on three of the Spencer Davis Group's hits: "Somebody Help Me," "Gimme Some Lovin'," and "I'm a Man." In addition to penning Traffic's

1

biggest hit, our soon-to be-released second effort included a song of mine called "Feelin' Alright?"

As much of a fan of The Beatles, Clapton, and Hendrix as I was then and now, I was an *enormous* Steve Winwood fan. His singing, his guitar, the organ and piano—all of it. I had always gone out of my way to see his performances. And here I was in a band with him and on my way to Blackwell's house for a Traffic meeting.

Not to say things with Winwood and the rest of the guys hadn't gotten … a little weird along the way. We had released our debut album the previous year to much acclaim. Just before it came out, however, I had shocked the band, the fans, the press, and, even to a degree, myself, by leaving Traffic. Crazy, right? I just wanted to make music. I didn't necessarily want to be a rock star.

But through a strange set of circumstances, I had reconnected with Traffic earlier in 1968, and now things seemed better and stronger than ever. We had just gotten back from the States where we had played some high-profile shows; we seemed poised for great things. At twenty-two years old, I had already bounced around a fair amount, and the stability of helping to continue to grow Traffic was something I was looking forward to. The timing seemed perfect, and I was thrilled about this next phase of the band.

As I got out of the car and rang the doorbell, I wondered how the next year would unfold. What plans was Blackwell masterminding for us? I was happy with the way my songwriting had developed on the second album and how, to me, the band sounded more cohesive. Traffic would, no doubt, be the ideal environment to keep striving and growing as an artist, to keep getting better. This was good. This was all very good.

I was met at the door by Blackwell's housekeeper, who led me into a spacious sitting room. It was quiet. No music was playing. Just a clock ticking somewhere in the vast, expansive home. The winter sunlight pouring into the room did little to warm it. On one side, sardined side-by-side-by-side on a couch, were my bandmates Jim Capaldi, Chris Wood, and Steve Winwood. There was no eye contact. No hearty greetings. No talking at all, in fact. Blackwell was standing casually off to the side. What the hell? This was not a normal meeting. Nobody was smiling. Though a fire was burning in the fireplace, the room was growing colder by the second. I took a seat directly opposite the guys in a solitary chair that seemed to be waiting for me.

"What's going on, guys?" I asked.

Steve got right to it. That soulful and distinctive voice that had trumpeted so many hit records and that I was such a fan of, replied, "Dave, I don't like the way you write, I don't like the way you sing, I don't like the way you play. And ..." he hesitated, "we don't want you in the band anymore."

My old pal Jim Capaldi could not, or would not, look at me. His eyes nervously darted down at the floor, then at Steve, then back down to his shoes. Same for Chris.

It was as though the ground had been pulled away from underneath me. Without uttering so much as a word, I got back in my car and drove back to my flat.

As the shock wore off, I became determined. It was going to take a whole lot more than Steve Winwood and a pair of fickle friends to make me turn away from music. Nothing could ever do that. In fact, as my practical, stubborn, won't-take-no-for-an-answer mind began to process what had just happened, I had the potent feeling that this grim event might further motivate me to make the music I wanted to make.

Had I just been fired? Or liberated?

Bird on the Wind

Some of us will have to lose, and some will have to win
But to know just where to go, you must know where you've been
Nothing ventured, nothing gained, there's nothing left to lose
Except to find out for yourself the things you always knew

If you want to fly high, like a bird on the wind
You've to give it, give it everything
If you want to fly high, like a bird on the wind
You've to give it, give it everything

Don't you think it's strange the way the mood can come and go?
One day you are riding high; the next you're riding low
Everyone has something special that is truly theirs
So to make the highest good, we all must learn to share

If you want to fly high, like a bird on the wind
You've to give it, give it everything
If you want to fly high like a bird on the wind
You've to give it, give it everything

Some of us will have to lose, and some will have to win
But to know just where to go, you must know where you've been
Nothing ventured, nothing gained, there's nothing left to lose
Except to find out for yourself the things you always knew

If you want to fly high, like a bird on the wind
You've to give it, give it everything
If you want to fly high like a bird on the wind
You've to give it, give it everything

CHAPTER TWO

Bird on the Wind

I was born David Thomas Mason in Worcester, the heartland of England, most would say, and it sure felt that way when I grew up there. Worcester is situated on the River Severn, some twenty-five miles south of Birmingham and twelve miles from the Welsh border. During my childhood, it was a town of about sixty thousand people, with as many pubs as there were days in the year. We were located just five miles west of Stratford-on-Avon and about twelve miles from Kidderminster, the stomping grounds of Led Zeppelin's Robert Plant and John Bonham. For those of you more classically inclined, the composer Sir Edward Elgar lived on the outskirts of town (his "Pomp and Circumstance" is a moving piece of music with a stirring melody that later became a patriotic song called "Land of Hope and Glory," the lyrics of which supposedly enraged Elgar greatly).

There's a magnificent cathedral that was built between 1084 and 1504. King John, who succeeded Richard I and signed the Magna Carta (which the US Constitution is based on), requested to be buried there. His tomb is the oldest royal effigy in England. Most effigies portray their subjects in their youthful prime of life, but King John's depicts him as he was at the time of his death, which came at forty-nine years of age. He looked so old to me when I was a kid. In retrospect, of course, he wasn't old at all. I mean, from my view of life at seventy-seven, he was practically just getting started. There is one section of the city called the Shambles that dates back to the War of the Roses.

Worcester hosts one of the finest cricket grounds in England and is home to Royal Worcester Porcelain, the oldest (or second-oldest, depending on whom you're talking to) porcelain maker in England. You should also be aware that this is the city where Worcestershire sauce originated, better known as Lea & Perrins. What struck me growing up in Worcester, most of all, wasn't any of these facts as much as the verdant green countryside where I spent most of my time running through the fields and swimming in the river, lost in stories I'd heard and read—*Alice in Wonderland* among my favorite of them.

We lived five miles outside town in a brick two-story home on a private country lane called Packington Road. I was born in the upstairs bedroom, all eleven and a half pounds of me, around three o' clock in the morning on the tenth of May in 1946. My mother, Nora Lillian Mason,

was thirty-eight years old, and my father, Edward Mason, was fifty-two. My father, I'm told, had summoned the doctor by walking to his house, which was not far away, and had awakened him by throwing stones at his bedroom window. "Dr Spaulding! He's coming! He's coming!"

Dad, born on May 9, 1894, was one of eleven children. His father—my grandfather, whom I never met—was a horse trader. He was also a heavy drinker and notorious for it. The story goes that the police came for my grandfather for some reason or another, and it took three officers to put him in the paddy wagon—which, in those days, was horse-drawn—whereupon my grandfather proceeded to punch his fist through the side of said transportation.

Life in those days was not easy for Dad. My grandfather once locked the entire family out of the house in the middle of winter, and, one night, very drunk, wrung the necks of some pigeons my father kept as pets. All this abuse and the strain of raising eleven children likely led to my dad's mother dying at the age of forty-six.

At eleven, Dad left school and went to work for British Railways, and at around the age of eighteen he went to fight at the Salonica front (also known as the Macedonian front) during 1914–18 in World War I. He was in transportation, driving trucks, and in those days, they had solid rubber tires—this was before the advent of pneumatic rubber tires—so a bumpy ride, no doubt. It was a metaphor for his life, for so many of our lives.

Since Dad had spent so much time around horses, it was only natural that he should have some of his own. He had a few, including some racehorses at one point. He spent a good part of his life at the track and was a member of nearly every course in England. A significant amount of my younger years were spent at the track with him. He could count among his

friends some of the finest trainers and jockeys, not to mention owners and bookmakers—the latter being individuals who made book on their own, which in England is legal. Unlike in America, betting continues throughout the entire race, even one or two furlongs from the winning post. This is where my father made money. These bets were made verbally, and accounts were settled at the end of the month. My father's word was his bond; no contracts or handshakes were necessary. He also owned a candy store for some forty-six years, which, much to my mother's chagrin, I'm sure, was open 364 days a year, closing only on Christmas Day. To add to this, he also had a small factory that made ice cream.

Despite all the sweets that surrounded him, my father was stern. This was exemplified, if not exacerbated, by the fact that he was not a man of many words. As for my own experience, I'll say it was somewhat unusual in those days to have a dad a lot older than my friends' fathers. Maybe it was age, maybe it was something else, but for whatever reason, we weren't very close, although I always had a great deal of respect for him.

My mother, Nora, on the other hand, was an enormous presence in my life. If not for her, I might not have ended up doing what I do for she was determined to let me develop without the dictates of my father. What a wonderful woman, even though she whaled on me once or twice, which I'm quite sure was needed. I was a headstrong, willful child. I was determined to have things my way. I appreciated Mom's no-nonsense approach to life and marveled through my life about her impressive ability to perceive the character of a person upon first meeting. This came in handy later in life when I'd bring her on the road with me for several rock and roll tours.

My father drove a car called a Lea Francis, which was a hand-built saloon car. One of his friends from horse racing was the man who owned the company. As a gift, when I was five, I received an exact replica of an old racing car, which was big enough for me to sit in and drive around. When I wasn't playing with it, which wasn't very often, we stored it in the hayloft above the stables at our house. One afternoon, impatient to wait for my parents to get it for me, I endeavored on my own into the barn and crawled up the ladder to attempt to lower my car to the ground so I could play with it. I lost my balance and fell onto the concrete floor. Nobody gave it much thought until a few weeks passed and my father noticed I was dragging my left leg behind me as I walked.

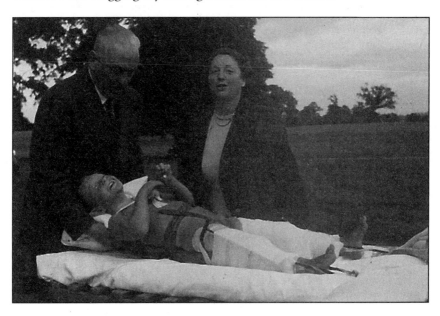

Concerned, my parents secured the best possible orthopedic doctor in England and sent me to a hospital in Oswestry called Aston Hall, an old, converted, stately home on twenty acres with two lakes and its own church. My hip wasn't broken; it was bent, a condition known as Perthes Hip. The remedy for this was to be strapped to a metal frame with both legs pulled taut so there was no movement in my legs and lower body for eight months. I endured a lot of injections in my legs and just as many enemas. My parents came to visit once a week, but most of that time I was on my own with the medical staff and a hospital full of other child patients. My parents brought candy from the store for me and some of the other children. The generosity and attention I got from my parents would backfire on me through one of the kids, who was deprived and, I guess, a little jealous. We were all strapped and immobilized in beds, but he would gather some of the other kids and verbally torment me.

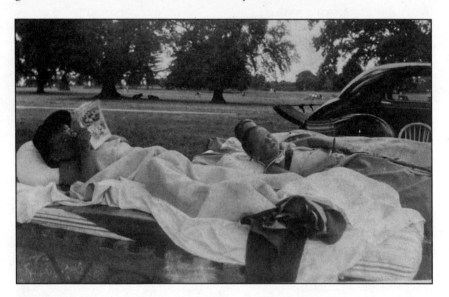

A remedy that nurses employed for misbehaving was to put us all behind the small church on the property, where we were left in solitude for hours. I had done nothing wrong, I wanted to insist; I was just being swept up in the bad behavior of the others, I suppose. (How badly you could misbehave strapped to a metal frame is beyond me.) Alone, behind that church at that age, was more bewildering than terrifying.

After the metal frame was removed, I had to learn to walk again. This took another six months of daily therapy, and *this* was terrifying— way scarier than being left strapped in bed and left behind a church. I remember I had to learn to stand on my own two feet, and I remember being frightened of letting go of a wall. There was some trouble between my parents at home, apparently, because I was left at Aston Hall for well over a month after my release and hadn't seen my parents for I can't be quite sure since I was so young, but by all accounts, it had been several months. Finally, I was returned home to Worcester by ambulance, on my own, which was a bittersweet ending to this life episode because I couldn't remember where we lived. It took a while to find our home.

I had a sister, Valerie, who was seventeen years older than me. She didn't live with us; she lived with my grandmother, who raised her. My parents weren't married when they had Valerie, and in those days, it was dealt with differently.

I didn't even know she was my sister until I was around nine years old, and Valerie moved to America. I wanted her to take me with her. I didn't really know what America was or what it was like, but I knew it was my destiny. I was always dreaming of greener pastures, no matter how green *ours* was. I wanted something other than my life as an only child, even though, since I came along rather late in life, I was spoiled. Rotten. My dad was often away at the races, and my mother was working at the candy store eight days a week until eight o' clock at night or later. I was left to my own devices and could do practically anything I wanted (though I did suffer from severe migraines as a child that would frequently curtail my free time activities).

So I had a lot of time on my own, not only because I was the only child at home and my parents were gone most of the time but also because we lived on a private road that had only two houses. The other house was occupied by a family named Randall. Mr. Randall owned and operated the local tan yards where hides were cured and turned into leather. He had a daughter named Susan, a pretty little blonde I remember teasing and taunting, as one does with a young crush, chasing her around and trying to pull her pigtails. (Be forewarned: She returns later in life in a six-degrees-of-separation story.)

Our house was situated on an acre of land. I truly grew up farm-to-table, as my parents grew apples, pears, plums, tomatoes, raspberries, strawberries, gooseberries, beautiful roses, and every green kind of vegetable imaginable. My father would spend hours making pickled mushrooms. Both of my parents were great cooks, and to this day I've never tasted an apple or blackberry pie like my mother could bake. Game birds were left hanging from the stable till the maggots broke them down enough to cook for dinner. Sunday dinner would be roast beef and Yorkshire pudding, with horseradish grown in the garden, so pungent it brought tears to my mother as she ground it by hand.

On the other side of the wall, at the bottom of the garden, was a large farm with cornfields, apple orchards, and hundreds of chickens. Fresh eggs were not a problem. This, and the surrounding countryside, was my playground, very much a Tom Sawyer existence. While I had friends I played with, most of the time I preferred to be alone—something I'd gotten good at since my days at Aston Hall.

Yet, in other ways, I never did feel quite on my own after returning to Worcester from Aston Hall.

One afternoon, after coming in from a day of adventuring in the fields, I returned to my house, empty as usual. As I walked through the living room and past the fireplace, I glanced up the stairs to see what can only be described as a presence. A gray-white, shadowy figure stood there. Just *stood* there. I wasn't startled, and I wasn't scared. Obviously, there were no words, but there was a clear message, a true knowing, that I was never really all alone, that I was loved and cared for. I was protected. I've carried this guardian angel with me my whole life.

Eventually, my legs were strong again, and I was able to return to school. I couldn't really walk long distances, so I rode a maroon-colored three-wheel tricycle to attend Henwick Grove Primary School, which served ages five to eleven. This was essentially a broad education in many subjects.

Henwick Grove Primary School, Mr. Arthur's class. I'm in the front row on the far right.

Discipline was quite strict, and there were a number of times that I was up before the headmaster, Mr. Platt. During these moments, he would usually administer the cane five or six times across each palm. There was one time when a boy named Edmund Dunn and I had to go up before Mr. Platt and receive our punishment. I'll never forget him coming out with his hands cut open. Though this seems extreme, I don't think it scarred me. My hands seem to work just fine as I play guitar. And I probably deserved it. As I said, I could be a handful.

In the back of all our heads was the vague threat of war. We kids had been raised with "duck and cover" drills throughout our youth, and conscription (the UK version of a military draft) was in effect through 1960. We all thought that maybe, at some point, we'd be off to battle. It was all vivid; I remember food rationing. I still have memories of seeing bombed-out buildings in many cities I'd visit when I traveled around England with my father. War wasn't something on TV. It was life right in front of our eyes.

On the beach with my mother and sister Valerie

I was in the Army Cadets and Air Force Cadets for a brief time when I was fourteen or fifteen, long enough to fall in love with planes. What captured me was the thought of flying, of freedom, really. I had been building model airplanes since I was nine, and I'd often take off by myself to parts of the countryside, not too far from Worcester, for an air show— either model planes, or full-size, real-world aircraft. I wanted to be a pilot. I wanted to fly. I wanted more than anything to be in the Royal Air Force.

There was just one catch: to complete this plan, I had to pass A-level exams in math, English, chemistry, and physics. Unfortunately, my math skills were never good enough.

I left school at sixteen and found another way to fly: the guitar.

And it started in a trash can.

In 1958, at age twelve, I journeyed to America with my mother to visit Valerie. This was a great adventure for me. We traveled on the Queen Elizabeth cruise ship to New York and then went by plane to California.

With my mother aboard the Queen Elizabeth on our way to America!

In those days, flying was a special experience where you dressed up. It took seven hours on a Pan American DC7. I, being a plane freak, loved it. Valerie was living in San Diego with her husband, Burt Leonard. There was so much to be impressed by: the weather, Disneyland (which had opened a mere three years earlier), and the Thunderbird that Burt drove.

What really dazzled me, though, was that were so many channels to choose from on the television. I mean, in England all we had was BBC and ATV—two stations! They didn't start until four or five in the afternoon, and they were over by midnight!

Equally, if not more impactfully, was the amount of rock and roll music that was played on the radio. I'd always loved music. We had a small collection of records, 78s, where I got my love for melody thanks to The Platters ("Only You," "The Great Pretender," "My Prayer"); Glen Miller ("In the Mood," "Wood Choppers Ball," "Moonlight Serenade," "String of Pearls"); George Formby, an excellent entertainer from the days of vaudeville ("Leaning on a Lamppost," "When I'm Cleaning Windows"); Flanagan and Allen, also from the vaudeville days ("Underneath the Arches," "Strolling"); and many others. The music from my parents' era may have sounded stale to my mates, but I enjoyed it thoroughly.

Fate struck while at my sister's. I was rummaging around outside and found a ukulele in a trash can. It only had three strings on it, and I had no idea how to tune it, but I banged away on that thing constantly. It was my first stringed instrument.

One afternoon, after using the bathroom, the toilet stopped up. I yelled, "Mum! The toilet needs unblocking!"

She replied, "Use the ukulele!"

To my dismay, my sister actually did—and without hesitation. Evidently, my first attempts at playing music were not well received.

I continued to be fascinated with the guitar after my short-lived ukulele experience. Once we were back in England, my idol became Hank Marvin, who was with a band called The Shadows, an instrumental rock group that also backed up Cliff Richard. I used to come home after school and listen for hours. My mother bought me my first guitar, a Mayfair, and I tried to mimic Marvin's playing style. I even started taking the guitar to school.

I'd come home and listen to records, trying to figure out how to play the parts. I was becoming totally self-taught by listening to records. These would either be a single, which were played at 45 RPM, or an LP, which were 33 RPM. The RPM, of course, stands for revolutions

per minute, and a turntable could go as slow as 16 RPM. I mention this
because it was very useful when trying to learn a new phrase or guitar
lick. You could slow the single down to 33 RPM and the LP to 16 RPM.

Eventually, I became a fan of The Ventures, Duane Eddy, a group called
The Hunters, The Outlaws, and Johnny and the Hurricanes. I couldn't get
enough of the guitar-driven instrumentals. I had found my passion, and I
was going to let it flow through me like a river.

You Can All Join In

Here's a little song you can all join in with
It's very simple and I hope it's new
Make your own words up if you want to
Any old words that you think will do, yeah

Yellow, blue, what'll I do?
Maybe I'll just sit here thinking
Black, white, stop the fight
Does one of these colors ever bother you?

Here's a little dance you can all join in with
It's very simple and I hope it's new
Make your own steps up if you want to
Any old steps that you think will do

Left, right, don't get uptight
Keep in line and you'll be alright
Clap hands, move around
Make sure no one puts you down

Here's a little world you can all join in with
It's very simple and I hope it's new
Make your own life up if you want to
Any old life that you think will do

Love, you, it's nothing new
There's someone much worse off than you are
Help me set them free
Just be what you want to be

Here's a little song you can all join in with
It's very simple and I hope it's new
Make your own words up if you want to
Any old words that you think will do, yeah

CHAPTER THREE

You Can All Join In

Like most children of my era, I first became interested in music because I heard my parents' records. My ukulele experience fascinated me because, while playing an instrument wasn't as easy as it looked, it sure was fun. It tapped into the same creative instinct as building airplane models. (How things are put together still piques my interest today.) Then I started singing in school choir and performing in plays. I also did Bible readings at school assemblies. I was, I suppose, finding my voice.

As a teenager, my fascination for performance grew, and I hungered for live music. I'd go as often as I could, meaning if a band with guitars in it was coming through town, I was there. I was intrigued, not only with the music itself but also with who was *playing* the music. What sort of people were these music makers? What were their lives like? I'd wait in the parking lot to catch a glimpse of these mysterious people, secretly hoping to meet band members, or even better, jump on the tour bus to garner an inside look.

Because I knew the manager of the local theater, he arranged for me to meet Little Richard backstage. I was about fifteen, and I couldn't believe this was really Little Richard in the flesh. Little Richard! The flamboyant gender-bender was chatty, but what I remember most was him looking me up and down with one raised eyebrow. Wonder what that was all about?

My fascination with music and those who made it grew as I grew, as if my love for melodies were a congenital defect that progressed with age. I saw The Beatles in 1963, with Roy Orbison opening, at a local movie house in my town called the Gaumont Cinema. In 1965, I saw The Rolling Stones there as well. I was at Royal Albert Hall in 1966 when Bob Dylan went electric. People lost their minds, accusing him of being "Judas" for daring to break out of his folkie persona, but I dug it. Who could imagine that, in a few short years, I would be in studios working with The Beatles, The Stones, and Dylan? Who in their wildest fantasies could ever imagine that? Certainly not me—and certainly not at fifteen.

There was nothing like the "Birmingham All-Nighters" concerts that went all the way to dawn. They would start at about 11:00 PM on Fridays and continue clear through to 7:00 AM Saturday mornings. The Birmingham Town Hall, where they were held, was a classic, epically historic place. On the same stage where Charles Dickens gave public readings to raise money and where Mendelsohn premiered *Elijah,* I got to see Brian Auger and the Trinity, featuring Ginger Baker; The Steampacket, featuring Judy Driscoll and a scratchy-throated warbler named Rod Stewart; John Mayall and the Bluesbreakers with Eric Clapton; The Lovin Spoonful at the Marquee; and scores of other bands.

I also saw Manitas De Plata, who was like the Jimi Hendrix of the flamenco guitar and the forerunner of The Gypsy Kings. His show at the Royal Albert Hall was life shaping for me as it convinced me, once and for all, of the power of the guitar. The PA failed that night, so De Plata used the hall's natural acoustics to deliver a spellbinding, unplugged performance. I was riveted.

Seeing live music was everything for me; it inspired me to forge ahead in music and encouraged me to be courageous enough to do it in my own style. My future career wasn't going to be as a Royal Air Force pilot. I wanted to be a guitar player. That was the life.

The first major step on my path toward this fate was starting my own instrumental guitar band. We called ourselves The Jaguars. I was sixteen. The members were Roger Moss on drums, Michael Mann on rhythm guitar, Dennis Morgan on bass guitar, and yours truly on lead guitar. As I've said before, my main inspiration was Hank Marvin of The Shadows. His sleek look, that red Strat, those expert guitar licks—I wanted to *be* Hank Marvin. I did my best to mimic him and the music of The Shadows and, to a great extent, The Ventures as well. We Jaguars? We were actually good enough to score paying gigs, which, as a young teenager in Worcester, meant we played weddings and a lot of pub dates.

I would have stayed an instrumental guitar player because, for me, the voice got in the way of music. But to get hired and secure more engagements, we had to put vocals into our show—specifically, recreating the current hit records of the time.

None of us could really sing, but we learned as we went along. That's what you do when you love what you're doing, and I loved music, so I began to sing, albeit reluctantly. I never intended to be front-and-center on stage. I just wanted to play my guitar and jam with my friends.

Our hard work and heart's calling paid off, though, and The Jaguars earned some local notoriety. We even released a single in 1963, "Opus to Spring," musically motivated by the classic. We recorded it at the local

MAJESTIC
CORN MARKET, WORCESTER

GRAND RE-OPENING NIGHT
TUESDAY, SEPTEMBER 3rd
WITH A
TEEN BEAT SPECTACULAR
INTRODUCING THE DYNAMIC
★ **MAL RYDER and THE SPIRITS** ★
AND WORCESTER'S OWN DISCOVERY
★ **THE JAGUARS** ★
Be with the beat from 7.45—10.45 p.m.
Admission FREE by ticket only
OBTAINABLE FROM THE MAJESTIC

YMCA where we rehearsed. I got a bunch of mattresses to isolate the instruments, and we recorded live on a two-track Grundig tape machine. Considering we were just a group of teens pursuing our passion in an endeavor that I now know is plenty difficult to accomplish, we were pretty successful locally. A local record store owner pressed the disc for us on a label created for the release called Impression Records, and he helped hustle it around town.

We didn't last too long, maybe a year. It all just sort of fizzled out. But not for me. I was in it for the long haul. Of that I was certain.

There was a band that would occasionally come and play in Worcester called The Sapphires. I liked them as a group, but it was the lead singer who really grabbed my attention.

His name?

Jim Capaldi.

At the time, Jim was doing a very respectable version of Elvis, complete with tight pants, a white jacket, a black shirt, and a pink tie. The Sapphires were from a neighboring town named Evesham, about twelve miles from Worcester. They would occasionally play at the Gaumont Theater, the same spot where I'd seen The Beatles and The Stones. I had become the DJ there when I was about sixteen, and every Saturday morning we would enjoy

Me and Jim Capaldi before our Traffic days

records and a movie, followed by a live band. To kick off our Saturday mornings, there would be a little rah-rah song that would come up with words on the movie screen and music through the sound system. We'd all sing along together to:

We come along on Saturday morning
Greeting everybody with a smile
We come along on Saturday morning
Knowing that life's worthwhile
As members of the GB Club we all intend to be
Good citizens when we grow up
And champions of the free
We come along on Saturday morning
Greeting everybody with a smile

I looked forward to Saturday mornings. It was such good fun for our community of fifty or so boys and girls. If Jim and his band were there, we'd go to Honky Fletcher's afterwards for fish and chips and mushy peas.

There was great rivalry between the local area bands as to who was the best. People would drift from one band to another trying to find that winning combination. As it turned out, Jim Capaldi had a natural ability as a drummer, and we eventually got together along with another friend, Gordon Jackson, on guitar, and David Meredith on bass. We became The Hellions. Prior to The Hellions, Jim, Gordon Jackson, and I briefly had a band called The Deep Feeling. (I'm not sure what we were trying to convey with that name.)

The Hellions started as a local Worcester band, playing at pubs, mainly, like The Lakes, where, incidentally, I saw Tom Jones before he became famous. He's always been a great singer. But The Hellions broke out of being just a hometown act and began to play in bigger and more established markets like Birmingham. After some trips to London, we secured management by a man named Morris King—a reasonably important music industry manager. This helped us immensely in terms of status and exposure. King managed two American brothers called The Walker Brothers who were popular in England and Europe. Under his management, we got a record deal at PYE Records, a label of some note. We chose to do a song by Jackie DeShannon called "Day Dreaming of You," DeShannon being an American girl who had written a number of hit songs. Our record was produced by an interesting character named Kim Fowley who had done a well-known novelty record called "They're

(Above) The Hellions (L-R) David Merideth, Gordon Jackson, me, and Jim Capaldi.

Coming to Take Me Away." For a boy fresh up from the country, Kim was genuinely a study in contradictions. I'd never seen anything like him and wasn't sure what to make of his androgynous ways but chalked it up to this newfound wild and wondrous thing called the music business.

"Daydreaming of You" never really took off. So, what to do next? We were introduced to an artist named P. J. Proby, who had landed a number of hit records in England, including "Hold Me." Now, this guy could really sing. Similar to Elvis, but better—way better. The Hellions were chosen to do a tour of England as P. J.'s backing band. It was a break.

But not only could this guy sing, this guy could drink. One night, I think it was at a theater in Wales, we started the set with him, and it became apparent that he'd had too much to drink—as in, *waaaaay* too much to drink. Before he could fall down, one of the stagehands brought out a chair, which he placed right at the foot of the stage. Proby was guided to the chair, and, thank God, sat down. He proceeded not to sing but to curse and swear at the audience.

These were the early days of rock and roll; this was not acceptable or normal, and the room was in a complete state of shock—not to mention us guys in the band. We were standing back there with our heads hung

low holding our instruments, wishing that one of those big platforms that bring people up through the stage floor would suddenly and magically swing into action and lower us somewhere down, away from view of the audience. We just wanted to disappear.

What was this thing called touring? What was the image I'd prefer to project? What sort of musician and band and performer identity did I want to craft? I was learning many lessons, firsthand, from hard-won experiences on the road.

Timing is everything, and I thank my lucky stars every day that my formative years as an artist happened during what is now called "Swinging London."

Swinging London was a phrase that became popular in 1966 to describe the cultural eruption that occurred in the city in the 1960s. It was a phenomenally creative wave that celebrated the young, the new, and the modern. A cultural revolution spawned in part by the recovery of the British economy after World War II, it was defined by equal parts optimism and hedonism. It also became fantastically overwhelming for musicians, fashion designers, models, photographers, and the like. There was no better place to be than London at that time.

The area in Soho around Carnaby Street, W1, and Kings Road, Chelsea was ground zero of this new surge of artistry. The British flag became a universal symbol of the swinging '60s, bolstered in part by England's home victory in the 1966 World Cup. And I was smack dab in the middle of it.

Jim Capaldi and I were roommates and bandmates in The Hellions and were, therefore, hanging out a lot. When we would play in Birmingham, one of our usual haunts was a nightclub called the Elbow Room. It wasn't a large lounge by any means, but it was the place to see and be seen, have a drink, listen to some music, check out the good-looking women, and maybe even score some hashish.

The club was owned by a man named Don Carlos and a West Indian named Roy, whose last name escapes me. Don Carlos was a hyper, neurotic man, while Roy was laid back and a very sharp dresser. Both were deeply steeped in music, especially jazz and the blues, so they encouraged musicians and singers to feel comfortable there. We got VIP treatment, like free drinks, and were always welcomed. They opened a second place in my hometown of Worcester called The Flamingo, and Jim and I played in the basement there on a regular basis. It was a cool place, not unlike the famed Cavern Club of Liverpool.

The Elbow Room was a hub for any of the top musicians playing in the area, including Steve Winwood, he of The Spencer Davis Group fame. It was his hometown. I'll never forget the first time I heard the Birmingham-based Spencer Davis Group on the radio. I liked them so much that I sought them out to hear them live in concert. In 1965, they were sharing bills with The Graham Bond Organization, John Mayall & The Bluesbreakers, and The Yardbirds, all of which were good bands. Standing out above them all, for me, was Winwood, Spencer Davis's extraordinary fifteen-year-old lead singer. I was drawn in instantly.

While enjoying his massive success, Steve started to be drawn to other musicians outside the Spencer Davis Group. It was at the Elbow Room where Jim and I began our relationship with Winwood and Chris Wood, a friend of Steve's and a self-taught flautist (and later saxophonist) who'd been a student at the Royal Academy of Art. Amid this scene, the four of us would get together as often as we could to hang out, get stoned, and listen to music.

The Hellions, despite our bold name, was basically out of steam. For a while I played guitar with a guy named Don Covey, whose real name was

Phil Canora, a phenomenally good drummer who had designs on being a lead singer. Not much was happening with that band, so during this time I started working as a roadie for the Spencer Davis Group. I did so along with a guy named John Glover. We didn't do much but set up amps and guitars. For me, it was really just an excuse to be able to hang out with the superb Steve Winwood.

One night, The Spencer Davis Group was playing a show outside of London, and Steve was a no-show. It was a sold-out house, and the rest of the band didn't know what to do. Spencer came over to me and said, "Dave, can you sing and play in Steve's place?"

My reaction was shock. But Spencer kept urging me, "Come on, I know you can." Because of Spencer's confidence in me, I thought just maybe I could pull it off. On the other hand, I was scared out of my mind—I mean, these people in the audience were expecting to see the boy wonder, the great Stevie Winwood. What the hell was going to happen when someone nobody's ever heard of was up there taking his place? Everybody in the band and crew prodded me, though, and I finally agreed.

The moral of this crazy story, this tremendous turning point in my life? At some point you have to take action to pursue your dreams. You can't just wish things into existence.

So, I got up on stage. I sang the hits, and it was incredibly fun and hugely empowering. Once I got started, the music took over; it carried me. It always does. I know that now, but I learned the truth of the magic of music that night and have never taken it for granted since. That moment still stays with me because I actually pulled it off (in spite of myself).

The crowd was pleased enough, but the real takeaway wasn't about the crowd; it was internal. I had my first real taste of what it felt like to be "good." Accepted. That brief focus of everyone's energy was daunting, but I would be lying if I said it didn't intrigue me and ignite a desire to not only be a guitar player, but a *great* guitar player.

I got lucky again around this time, getting to sing background vocals on three Spencer Davis Group records that I mentioned earlier: "Somebody Help Me," "Gimme Some Lovin'," and "I'm a Man." And that's how it—at least the "it" of this particular era—all started.

Winwood was clearly getting tired of the Spencer Davis Group, tired of being called the "White Ray Charles." He was itching for a change.

One night backstage, he said as much to Spencer, who hit the roof in anger.

Back at the Elbow Room, Jim, Steve, Chris, and I continued to hang, bond, dream, and start thinking that maybe there was a band in us. It was just a concept, then. We never played any place, maybe just jammed a bit. But the chemistry felt right, so we decided to try to start a band.

Of course, every band needs a name, and we needed something unique, something without the word "the" in front of it. Jim and I had gone to a movie matinee in Worcester, and as we were leaving the theater, which opened out to High Street, just as we were coming down the steps, Jim suddenly stopped and said, "I got the name." Looking at all the automobiles going up and down the street, he turned toward me with a smile and said, "Traffic."

And that was it. It was that simple. And it was brilliant.

Jim and I knocked around a lot together and shared a lot of fun memories. In March of 1967, we went to see The Who at the Malvern Winter Gardens, just outside of Worcester. We knew a couple of the roadies, so we were able to get in easily.

Problem was, The Who didn't show up. The place was packed; people couldn't even move. You could feel them getting restless, so one of the roadies said to me and Jim, "You guys get out there and play."

What? Well, we did.

With Jim on Keith Moon's drums and me on Pete Townsend's guitar, all we were missing was a bass. I announced to the crowd The Who was a no-show and asked if anybody played a bass guitar. Sure enough, somebody took me up on my offer and climbed onstage. We played a few songs and, in tribute to the missing Who, smashed Townsend's guitar and, with the help of the crew, kicked Keith Moon's drums all over the stage.

I'm sorry I missed a chance around this time to meet Bob Dylan (though it would happen years later, several times). He had played in London and wanted to meet Winwood, who was now, of course, putting a new band together. Dylan and his entourage went off to meet Steve, Jim, and a few others in the midnight hour at a place called Witley Court just on the outskirts of Worcester. This was one of those truly magnificent old estates, which, in its height of opulence during the Victorian era, hosted lavish parties attended by nobility, prominent artists, and all manner of influential people. The rumor is that the master of the house had taken it into his head that the grand place should be burned to the ground. Be it true or false, that's exactly what happened, for in 1937, a fire all but devastated it, leaving behind only a shell of its former glory.

Local lore is rampant with gossip of hauntings. We would often go out there at night and look for ghosts, but I regret I missed meeting Dylan when he was there that night.

Rock and roll is also full of lore, and truth be told, I didn't have much self-awareness then, which is the real distinction between myth and truth. I was aware that music was embedded in my soul, that it was as imperative of a part of me as my blood and cells. But I was also a teenaged boy. In writing this book, I thought it might be wise to get an outside look on who I was at that time.

Carol Smith is Dave's cousin, the daughter of Grace, Dave's mother Nora's sister. She is the last living relative in England of his generation. Carol and Dave spent many childhood moments together in Worcester, England.

Carol Smith:
David and I met, I would say, when we were five or six. We had a wonderful time growing up in Worcester. David got up to lots of mischief (I called it fun!). At times, it really got him in deep shit. That was just David—always pushing things to the limit, and then a bit beyond. I remember when my family had just moved into a

new house. I think Dave was around twelve. My mum was up a ladder painting the guttering with black gloss paint. David and I came around, and David said, "You shouldn't be doing that. I will do it for you." Mum came down the ladder, and David went up, black paint in hand. He was getting on fine but suddenly lost his footing, and the black paint was all down the new brick work and all over Mum. David and I didn't know whether to laugh or cry. Mum was not amused, as you can imagine. It took years to get the paint off the bricks.

My father, Ted Mason, was a prisoner of war in the Second World War, and at the camp he was in, he entertained his buddies by putting on shows. He always raised a smile. Ted and David's other half-brother, John, and their father, Edward Mason, all had somewhat of the ham in them! David, as a young person, was somewhat solitary. He only communicated with whom he wanted and when he wanted—a bit like me.

David's main interest in music, as I remember, came after he left Henwick Grove School, at age eleven. He went to that school because it was close to his home, which was helpful because of his hip. I don't think he and the headmaster "gelled," shall we say. Later, I went to wherever David was playing if I could. The Hellions is my first recollection of a band name, but I believe there was one before that. I'm guessing he was fourteen or fifteen, but they were just wonderful. I loved his jamming, guitar playing, and practicing. I felt he had real talent and would go a long way. You could just feel that he was taking it quite seriously.

A venue David played at many times was a public house called The Lakes. It was located in quite a rough council housing estate, but there was never ever any trouble, maybe because of the bouncers at the door. Each gig they did was absolutely full to the gunnels.

One time, David's mum turned up to see him play—that just never happened before. I can't tell you how pleased we all were that she came because my mum and dad never came to see him. I remember Nora was blown away by how good David was and how the crowd appreciated his music. How lovely it must have been for Dave. It was wonderful for me to see his face—just sheer joy.

Jim Forrester is a childhood friend from Worcester, England, where he still lives. He and Dave reconnected at Dave's tour in England in 2018 after many years.

Jim Forrester:

With Worcester being my place of birth, I have followed Dave's career for almost sixty years. My memories are genuine and given as witnessed by a fifteen-year-old lad, myself, back in the day in the City of Worcester.

The music scene was around 1963–64 in the UK and was moving on a pace. The City of Worcester took part in this on a considerable scale. Every village hall would have a local band playing each weekend. Within thirty miles of the City of Worcester, famous bands were starting to make their way up the music ladder: Led Zeppelin, ELO, Black Sabbath, and The Moody Blues, to name a few. It is not surprising that the talented fourteen-year-old David Mason fancied a slice of the action. Dave hardly had time to leave Henwick Grove and Christopher Whitehead Secondary Modern before he was dreaming of becoming the next Hank Marvin and performing the classic Hank guitar solos "FBI," "Apache," and "Man of Mystery."

The Co-op Hall right in the middle of the City of Worcester was the place where the most popular Worcester Bands performed. Among the most popular was a group of young chaps who called themselves The Jaguars. When The Jaguars performed, the place was packed out, and they were very good. The stage uniform of the band was a very smart gray silver suit; they did look good. It was apparent that the real powerhouse of talent came from the guitar playing of Dave Mason. He gave us all The Shadows stuff. He was the frontman and did all the singing.

As time went on, I met Dave and a new mate of his, Jim Capaldi, who was from the nearby town of Evesham and who worked in a Worcester factory as an engineer. They would both frequent Worcester coffee bars The Cellars and The Flamingo, and we would play the jukebox and chat over espressos. It was disappointing for me when I read soon after that The Jaguars had disbanded. But the disappointment was short lived when I heard that Dave and Jim had joined forces with Gordon Jackson, John Palmer, and Dave Meredith, who had lived near Jim and who had previously played in a band The Cherokees. They, too, were very good. This new band was called The Hellions. With my own mates and girlfriends, I began to follow The Hellions whenever I could. Wowee, were they good! Dave shared frontman duties with the drummer at the back, Jim Capaldi. I can recall, particularly, seeing them at The Guildhall in Worcester. I can also recall thinking, "These local boys, one way or another, are going to make it."

I could tell of many other such gigs at The Flamingo, New Street, where The Hellions were regulars, and other Worcestershire venues, for the City of Worcester this was all too good to last, and The Hellions were off to London to perform in nightclubs. We'd hear stories of jam sessions at the famous Elbow Room when Dave and Jim met up with the young Steve Winwood and Chris Wood. These stories are now local legend. The City of Worcester had then lost David Mason; however, what a catalog of music we all gained.

Hole In My Shoe

I looked in the sky where an elephant's eye
Was looking at me from a bubblegum tree
And all that I knew was the hole in my shoe
Which was letting in water (letting in water)

I walked through a field that just wasn't real
With one hundred tin soldiers which stood at my shoulder
And all that I knew was the hole in my shoe
Which was letting in water (letting in water)

I climbed on the back of a giant albatross
Which flew through a crack in the cloud
To a place where happiness reigned all year 'round
And music played ever so loudly

I started to fall and suddenly woke
And the dew on the grass had soaked through my coat
And all that I knew was the hole in my shoe
Which was letting in water (letting in water)

CHAPTER FOUR

Hole in My Shoe

Steve Winwood was still unwinding his role in The Spencer Davis Group while we were discussing the formation of Traffic. There was, as I said, definite musical chemistry. Unlike most other bands, however, we had zero musical history together. We didn't play clubs. We didn't even perform cover songs to start. Traffic was an abstract idea—all gut and instinct. We had a feeling, and we wanted to explore it, discover if our chemistry was real.

After a few weeks of occasional jamming, we were still searching to land upon what we would be like as a unit. We all had diverse musical tastes and were, in a sense, what would now be called an "alternative band." This was all well and good, but we had no finished original material.

I looked upon this as an opportunity to write despite not yet having written anything up to that point. Jim and Steve were becoming a great team, with Jim writing lyrics and Steve putting music to his words. So that's when I started writing too.

We would be managed by Chris Blackwell, the man you met earlier and who, as I mentioned, signed us to Island Records. Blackwell had worked closely with Steve, and the rest of us were nobodies. The deal was a no-brainer.

Winwood was already a big name in the UK and Europe, for which I am eternally grateful because he gave us instant interest from the public and a certain guarantee of success.

And it wasn't unfounded. Winwood was the magnet that drew us together, the glue that *kept* us together—at least for a time.

That said, we certainly had to prove ourselves, and I wasn't going to let this opportunity go to waste. My then-girlfriend, Carol Russell, designed the now-famous four-armed wheel that became the Traffic logo, and we were off and running.

Sort of.

Where were we supposed to figure out our meaning and purpose? Where could we escape to figure out what we were or what we were to be?

We discovered the answers to these questions at the Berkshire Cottage, a remote, two-story farmhouse far outside London in the parish of Aston Tirrold. We found the location through Blackwell and through *his* relationship with a man named William Pigott Brown, who owned a large thoroughbred racing stable there.

The land in Berkshire, in the valleys between Oxford and London, is where the tribes of the Stone Age and Bronze Age settled, farmed, and built their monuments—mainly giant earthworks like Silbury and Uffington. This land has mystical power and energy, and we were all about that.

Our rustic cottage was situated just five minutes from these ancient settlements, and some of the most amazing, organic, raw, and innovative musical experiences of my lifetime happened in it. When we moved in, there was no electricity or running water. The toilet was outside in a wooden shed. But we were surrounded by beautiful rolling hills and natural open space, completely isolated. It wasn't a chance decision; it was a calculated move. It was somewhere to be free to focus on the music, undisturbed.

We nailed Carol's original logo to the living room wall, threw some paint up, and took over what had formerly been called the Sheepcote Farmhouse. It was a very basic two-story structure with a slab roof and an exterior made of local clay and limestone. There was a dining area, a kitchen, a living room with a large fireplace, and four bedrooms upstairs. Since there was no electricity, we got a 100-watt generator behind the house to power our gear. The nearest phone was half a mile away, and the only running water was cold.

To get there from the main road, there was a two-tire track path. If it had been raining, it was a mud bath—four-wheel-drive time. We would often have to go pick up stranded visitors in a Willys Jeep—the powerhouse of an American Army vehicle that replaced horses and other draft animals during the Second World War. Later, we poured a concrete slab directly in front of the house. At first, we would use this as a place to park vehicles, but it took on a far more important function: When the weather was pleasant, we would set up our gear right out in nature and just blast away. It became our first stage.

The main space downstairs was completely set up for music. Steve positioned his organ in the corner facing the drums. Saxophones, amplifiers, and guitars were strewn all over the place, and the low ceiling and heaps of natural wood helped absorb the musical vibrations.

Our official move-in date was April 1, 1967. From the beginning, there was lots of talk about the place being haunted, at least among the other guys. I never felt it, but they talked about the shadows, sounds, and other anomalies a lot. Looking back, it's easy to wonder if perhaps the large amounts of hashish and other things we were ingesting may have been affecting them—us.

Jam sessions would usually commence in the early evenings and sometimes last all night. I can remember lying in bed as the sun was coming up and hearing Chris outside playing his flute among the birds, making their morning calls.

The cottage was a transformative, if somewhat rugged, experience. A guy we knew named Albert Heaton became our roadie. He had a large van that was painted pink, and our arrow symbol was soon stenciled on the side. We would chop wood for fires on cold days. There were no distractions, just hundreds of acres around us, green-covered hills curling out to infinity where they would bring the horses from Piggott Brown's stables for their workouts every day. We would sit around, smoke hash, and noodle on acoustic instruments.

Being isolated from authority, or an actual audience, was powerful. We made music by candlelight.

We also wandered. We were spontaneous, doing things like going in search of a bedframe that Winwood wanted, which was stored away in a nearby abandoned cottage (or so we thought). We jumped up from our jam session, got in Steve's old Willys Jeep, and mashed through the mud and soft hillsides with only our headlamps on until we got to the cottage. In the pitch-black interior, we located the bedframe and, while loading it out to the Jeep, were suddenly confronted by a crazy old man with a bright, glaring flashlight, who shrieked, "What are you doing?" We were completely surprised to know anybody else was on the land, and, flabbergasted, we dropped the bed and ran off in opposite directions. We all made our way back, eventually and miraculously, to our cottage where we just collapsed laughing at what almost seemed to be a ghost. We had many moments of genuine hilarity. We had many moments of brotherhood. Both made for great music.

Sometimes we'd go to the local pubs in nearby Wallingford to sip pints and play darts. Sometimes we just stayed home, and occasionally we'd drop acid. We smoked a lot of hash—did I mention that? The police and everybody else left us alone, which was fortunate because during this time in London, arrests were definitely happening. The Rolling Stones had been busted for drug possession at Keith Richards's famous Redlands estate just a couple of months earlier, which was huge news. But somehow, we managed to stay under the radar because we were in our own world in the middle of nowhere.

We installed some equipment in the cottage, which included a set of Bang & Olufsen reel-to-reel tape machines. Microphones were hung from the ceiling so our jams were captured all the time. I remember seeing boxes piling up, most of them labeled "Traffic jam." I wonder where those are today.

We'd soon have electricity and hot water, and the wild weekend parties (featuring film and music people, models, and good drugs) thrown at William Pigott Brown's estate provided just the right amount of distraction for us.

Out of all the jamming and stretching, little riffs and melodies would start coming to life, and Jim would start scratching out some lyrics. It was all very interactive. I might pick up a bass guitar, Steve might sit behind the drums, and Chris might get behind the organ while Jim picked up an acoustic guitar. We were getting into improvisation and playing lots of jazz throughout the house, including John Coltrane, Cannonball Adderley, Roland Kirk, Dizzy Gillespie, and Charles Lloyd. Additionally, there was a lot of international music being played, from Indian to Chinese, Bulgarian to African drum records, classical, the blues—it was a real musical stew. It was an amalgamation of everything fascinating and exotic: "world music" before the term existed.

Sequestering ourselves in the countryside was an unusual practice in those days. Most of the music was going on in London. While we were holing up in a rural cottage in the Berkshire Downs to write and rehearse for several months prior to recording, across the pond, interestingly enough, something similar was happening in a pink-colored house in upstate New York: The Band was ensconced. And three thousand miles west of The Band, The Grateful Dead's members were living together and making music in a shared San Francisco space. We were all experimenting, and unbeknownst to one another, we were, as a result of our communal habitats, collectively creating the "jam" movement.

A mythology about Traffic began forming as spring turned into the summer of 1967. We were something of a mystery, being out of the public eye but already having some established roots.

As we progressed, there was writing going on among all of us. I tended to keep to myself in that regard, though. I was still discovering what I was capable of as a songwriter. I didn't think it was a big deal because, conceptually, this was a band that should have been able to handle anything, from writing in teams to working individually.

Meanwhile, in London, in the spring of 1967, The Beatles were working on what would become what I still consider the best concept album ever made, *Sgt. Pepper's Lonely Hearts Club Band*. It was an amazing time to be in music. Traditional barriers were being broken, even thrashed and dismantled and put back together—again, a different kind of concept that I'd been enthralled with since I was a child. It was a time when we all supported one another and encouraged creativity. The Beatles, obviously, were a constant source of inspiration; they were coming out with new music all the time.

The first Beatle I met was Paul McCartney. I was still with Carol Russell at the time, a gifted design artist and graduate of the prestigious London Royal College of Art. She had the run of every department, she was that talented. McCartney commissioned her to make, of all things, a transparent couch in which all the characters from the songs on *Sgt. Pepper* were visible inside it. He came to her studio one evening to check on the progress. Since it was during one of my trips from the cottage to see Carol in London, I was there as well. Paul was open and very interested in what Traffic was doing. He was chatting about this new conceptual album. I don't recall exactly everything we talked about while he was there, but the fact that I was hanging with a Beatle, one of the greatest bass players of all time, and such an exceptional singer and songwriter, was one of those moments I'll always remember. After all, no matter what, I was—and still am—a fan. I, of course, didn't say no to Paul's invitation to visit Abbey Road.

This led to becoming friends with George Harrison, which led to an afternoon at George's house in Surrey, where he lived with Pattie Boyd. The place was staggering, starting from the outside, which, shortly after they moved in, they painted in wild and imaginative psychedelic patterns.

Traffic in the early days. You can see the band logo leaning against the keyboard.

Inside also had an artsy vibe; around the fireplace, there was a mural painted by the design collective known as The Fool (Simone and Marijke), whom I got to spend time with. They were famous in London for having painted the Apple Building, Harrison's Mini Cooper, and John Lennon's Rolls Royce. In the back of the house was a swimming pool in the shape of a guitar.

The afternoon I arrived, George was alone. We walked through the house, the walls covered with multiple awards and platinum records, reminding me I was in the presence of some of the best music around. Yet, to me, George's warm personality made everything feel natural and easy. We settled in his music room and sat on the floor, which was filled with inviting, colorful, ornate Indian throw pillows. Patchouli incense burned, and the lighting was soft and soothing. Harrison filled a bowl with hash.

"Would you like to hear the new record?" George asked.

"Absolutely," I said. "Of course." Who wouldn't want to hear the yet-to-be-released Beatles record with one of the people who actually created the music?

He carefully removed the shiny black acetate from an unmarked white sleeve and placed it on his state-of-the-art turntable. He dropped the needle, and my consciousness was shifted for the next nearly forty minutes as we listened to *Sgt. Pepper's Lonely Hearts Club Band*. That magical introduction, "Lucy in the Sky with Diamonds," "She's Leaving Home," "A Day in the Life"—the rules of music changed for me right then and there.

What made the album a gamechanger? Well, in addition to the musical genius of the four of them, recording techniques developed by the Abbey Road technicians gave The Beatles more than just the basic four-track equipment that had been in standard use. They stretched the limits and defied conventions of what were considered acceptable recording techniques. The way the songs on *Sgt. Pepper's* flowed from one to the next was another layer of studio innovation altogether. The Beatles had made use of the studio itself as an instrument. This was not merely a collection of songs. This was a huge, daring, collective idea, soon to be presented with equal visual panache with Peter Blake's artwork and the lyric sheet included in the gatefold sleeve.

It was impossible not to be swept away by the peerless production, much of it steered by the genius of their producer, George Martin. It was so good, in fact, that part of me thought, why bother making music anymore? Nothing could ever top this.

Ultimately, however, greatness, when embraced, is exhilarating. Music isn't a competition; it's something to celebrate.

"Within Without You" sparked a conversation with George about Indian music; we were both interested. That's when George got up and left the room, returning with a beautiful instrument in his hand. "Here, I want you to have this," he said. "It's the sitar I learned on." George was a truly generous spirit, and I made good use of his kind gift on the songs "Paper Sun" and "Hole in My Shoe."

After living and working together for a month or so out in the country, Chris Blackwell was pushing for us to get something out on the market, so we recorded a song written by Steve and Jim called "Paper Sun." Very psychedelic and poppy, very of the moment. Around that time, The Beatles had just broken ground with the concept of promo films after they shot something for "Strawberry Fields," and that inspired us to go to the Royal Museum for Central Africa in Belgium to shoot a film for "Paper Sun." It's a simple black-

and-white clip that shows us wandering among exhibits of the art and culture of the Congo. Meandering around, discussing displays, lots of skeletons and stuffed animals. It was cerebral and avant garde for the time. (Admittedly, to this day, I have no idea what it had to do with the music.)

In any event, maybe it helped our song because "Paper Sun" came in at number five on the British charts. This delighted us. (For reference, Procol Harum's "Whiter Shade of Pale" held the number one spot for thirteen weeks at the time.) To celebrate our number five placement, we rented a London club and invited all our friends. By the time we all rolled out of there in the wee hours of the early morning, we noticed a message scrawled on a dusty mirror in the lobby. We surrounded the mirror in a semicircle and got silent as we read the words, "Congratulations on your success, Paul McCartney." He had been there the whole time, but we had never even noticed him.

Soon after, a young American photographer named Linda Eastman came out to the cottage to shoot some pictures of us. She had come over from the States to photograph rock stars, and there was enough of a buzz about the cottage that she could not resist a visit, I suppose. You may recognize the name. Some of you? I'm sure you will. Eventually, Linda would go on to become Mrs. Paul McCartney.

After "Paper Sun," Blackwell was on us about a follow-up. The album would not be ready until the end of the year, we estimated, but we needed to continue putting out singles to keep the public interested.

I told the guys I had written a song on my own called "Hole in My Shoe." It was a childlike sort of fairytale, the first song I had ever written. Like I said, the story of Alice in Wonderland was something that captivated me as a child, and I thought and continue to think the imagery in the song reflects much of the sensibility that Lewis Carroll evoked. The song is part homage, part parody.

"Hole in My Shoe" caught the guys off guard. They did agree to record it, but they seemed to bristle all the way through, which created some tension in the studio, an off mood we weren't used to. They just seemed to hate the song. They thought it was way too commercial, a trite little ditty that didn't mean anything.

This is where I must give our producer Jimmy Miller a lot of credit. He kept the mood light and helped everything and everyone stay on track. I think the guys in the band hated it even more once it was done; they even wanted to scrap it. But when the marketing staff at Island Records heard it, they loved it. It was a guy at the label named Dave Betteridge who really got behind it, and that's all it needed. It was released as the next single and made it all the way up the charts to number two, selling more than 250,000 copies in the UK. Engelbert Humperdink's "The Last Waltz" kept me from a number one.

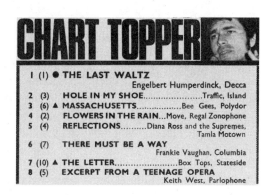

			CHART TOPPER	
1	(1)	●	THE LAST WALTZ	
				Engelbert Humperdinck, Decca
2	(3)		HOLE IN MY SHOE.....................Traffic, Island	
3	(6)	▲	MASSACHUSETTS.................Bee Gees, Polydor	
4	(2)		FLOWERS IN THE RAIN...Move, Regal Zonophone	
5	(4)		REFLECTIONS..........Diana Ross and the Supremes,	
				Tamla Motown
6	(7)		THERE MUST BE A WAY	
				Frankie Vaughan, Columbia
7	(10)	▲	THE LETTER.....................Box Tops, Stateside	
8	(5)		EXCERPT FROM A TEENAGE OPERA	
				Keith West, Parlophone

You would've thought a big hit would have been great news for the band, right?

Wrong.

While "Hole in My Shoe" was a hit critically and commercially, the other band members continued to absolutely despise it. The thing about it is that I knew the piece wasn't an illustrious composition; neither was anything else I was writing at the time. And they were all very much studio records, hard to reproduce live with what was available to us electronically at the time. I was learning, experiencing, searching, growing. I was, after all, only twenty years old when I wrote it.

But my sensibilities were certainly toward making hit records. Though the rest of the band might have looked at my early attempts as uncool, a hit record brings more attention. We all know that. It also attracts more people who would probably never hear the other music Traffic was making without a hit like the one I wrote.

But it's a fine line, of course. How do you create music that satisfies your inner muse while creating something that people will enjoy and ultimately buy? How do you bridge the sometimes-wide divide between commerce and art? The point of Traffic, I thought, was this: anything is possible. "Hole in My Shoe" put a spotlight on me that, up until then, had only been on Steve. I was toeing that fine line and proving that it could be done while also proving myself.

Despite my bandmates' dislike for "Hole in My Shoe," I gave a copy to Paul McCartney at his house in London one evening right before all four Beatles were flying off to Greece to negotiate the purchase of an island or something. A week or so later, I received a telegram saying, "Great record," that was signed by Paul, John, George, and Ringo. In the face of my own band's contempt for the song, I felt vindicated. The telegram? It's one of those things I've lost along the way, but I sure wish I'd kept it.

There were growing tensions in the band—in the recording studio at least. We could all feel it. Nonetheless, Jimmy Miller made everything easy. He was all about the Traffic vibe and made everyone feel comfortable and like we each belonged there. Jimmy was brought over from America by Chris Blackwell to produce Traffic and probably any other Island recording artist. (For the record—pun intended—he went on to produce the Stones' *Beggar's Banquet* at Olympic Studios.) And because of my association with Jimmy, I'd drop by the studio and listen to what was going on. That was not unusual at the time; we all were listening to each other recording. At one particular session, the song the Stones were working on was "Street Fighting Man." At some point, someone said, "Dave, why don't you come sit in with us?" And that's how I came to be on the song.

The basic track was put together in a fascinating way. Keith Richards wanted to get a sound on his acoustic guitar to replicate the highly compressed quality of recording on a small cassette machine. We sat around in a circle on the floor—Keith, Brian Jones, Charlie Watts, and me. Charlie had a little briefcase with a snare drum and a tiny cymbal in it. Brian and I had two large Moroccan drums, and Keith had the acoustic guitar that was feeding into a cassette player that, in turn, fed into a tape machine. That's how the basic track for "Street Fighting Man" was recorded. I later put the horn part on the fade-out of the song using a shehnai, another Indian instrument that I was learning and *kind of* knew how to play (it's a double-reed, oboe-like woodwind).

Incidentally, I loved what the Stones were doing on *Beggars Banquet.* To me, that was the album that really defined who and what they were. They had made a lot of solid records up until that point, but I don't think they had really evolved into the sort of group that would change the world the way they have. They were coming off an album called *Their Satanic Majesties Request,* which seemed, in part anyway, a clunky response to what The Beatles were doing with psychedelic music. But *Beggars Banquet* was different. It had the blues, but it was an evolution of the blues. It had some country, incorporating lots of truly American influences but done in the Stones' unique style. And I always felt a bit of a connection to the warm acoustic sounds on that record. After all, Mick Jagger had wandered over to Studio B one night where Jimmy Miller was producing our first Traffic album. That's part of what makes Mick so smart; he always had his ear up, staying connected to what was new and different. He must've really liked what he saw and heard Jimmy doing with us because that's how Miller began his long relationship with The Rolling Stones. One night at Olympic when I ran into Mick, I said to him, "This record you're making sounds phenomenal. It really feels like a huge next step for the band." He appreciated the observation.

One night, back at our band house, Jim Capaldi sat in front of the fireplace with a pen and paper and sketched a crude figure wearing a spiky hat with puppet strings attached. Next, he scribbled a short letter to "Mr. Fantasy." After Jim had crashed (as had I), Steve and Chris discovered the paper and started constructing a song. Jim's minimalist lyrics worked perfectly, and the next day we all got together to work up the song "Dear Mr. Fantasy." We knew it was great, so we called Jimmy and had him book us at Olympic Studios the next night. We were all excited as we hopped into the pink van for the trek back to London.

Eddie Kramer was the engineer, Chris was on the Hammond organ, Steve was on guitar, I played bass, and Jim was on the drums. But something wasn't right. We were working in the big room at Olympic that used large dampening screens to keep instruments from bleeding from one channel to another. We were all walled off and wearing headphones. We couldn't really feel one another, so it wasn't coming together right. This song was special, and we were missing the basic visual chemistry that we had at the cottage.

We knew what we had to do. We ditched the headphones and the screens and gathered close together as if we were back in the living room. We had no real ending to the song until Jimmy came out of the control room, picked up a pair of maracas, and got us to double the tempo. Then we knew we had it. It was not just a great song but the name of our debut album and a song that would come to characterize the band Traffic.

In September, before our big premier in London, a short tour was booked to get us ready for our official unveiling as a live band. The first show was in Oslo, and it was incredibly well-received. Our second show, in Stockholm, was recorded and broadcast on the radio. Listeners went crazy. "Hole in My Shoe" was a trip to play live because it began with me playing a long sitar introduction.

We were good live. Even just a couple of shows in, you could tell we were different. It was like there was no style we couldn't tackle, and the audiences seemed to grasp that. We did a short tour with The Who (they showed up) and several other bands, then we went to Gothenburg, Copenhagen, and Denmark, building up momentum until we reached London for our show at the Saville Theater on September 24. The tension was high, and the crowd was star-studded. Brian Jones was there, as were Eric Burdon, Cat Stevens, The Hollies, Paul McCartney, and many others.

We played our set, and the audience roared. McCartney loved us so much he called Island Records a couple of days later to say he wanted us to be in The Beatles' upcoming *Magical Mystery Tour* film. Shortly after, a film crew was dispatched to the cottage as we shot an early-form "video" for "Here We Go Round the Mulberry Bush," which we'd originally written and recorded as the title song for a comedy film. We were out on the Berkshire hilltop, marching around and pushing a twenty-foot-diameter earth balloon, each carrying a personal totem. Paul thought he might want to include it, but when *Magical Mystery Tour* came out on British television the day after Christmas, for some reason we were not included (thankfully, the footage still exists).

We toured with a couple of great new American bands, The Young Rascals and Vanilla Fudge. From London, we played Chesterfield, Newcastle, Liverpool, Croydon, then back home to Birmingham, followed by Bristol, Wolverhampton, and, finally, Ipswich. We did a bunch of BBC radio shows after that, and with less than a week break, we hit the road across England on a package tour with The Who, The Tremeloes, and The Herd.

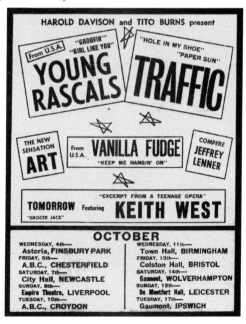

Fifteen tour stops and two shows a night. There were more BBC sessions in the middle of it all, and the terrific reviews of our shows continued. We were, ultimately, becoming stars.

But we still had an album to finish. As autumn became winter, we had one more song to record, "No Face, No Name, No Number," and then we were done with the music. It felt doable.

But what to do with the album cover? After smoking enough hash and going back and forth with ideas, we settled on the idea of Mr. Fantasy sitting in a room with us. Paul Medcalf, who was an art student and long-time friend of ours, volunteered to put on makeup and dress in character as we all sat nearby while a fire roared in the cottage's living room. The photographer, John Benton Harris, used a lens filter to achieve the garish, ruby-red glow.

We were done. The album was ready, and *Dear Mr. Fantasy* was soon released. A tour was set for America.

Then I quit the band.

Feelin' Alright?

Seems I've got to have a change of scene
'Cause every night I have the strangest dream
Imprisoned by the way it could have been
Left here on my own, or so it seems
I've got to leave before I start to scream
But someone's locked the door and took the key

You feelin' alright?
I'm not feelin' too good myself
Well, you feelin' alright?
I'm not feelin' too good myself

Well, boy, you sure took me for one big ride
And even now I sit and I wonder why
Then when I think of you I start to cry
Just can't waste my time, I must keep dry
Gotta stop believin' in all your lies
'Cause there's too much to do before I die.

You feelin' alright?
I'm not feelin' too good myself
You feelin' alright?
I'm not feelin' too good myself

Don't get too lost in all I say
Though at the time I really felt that way
But that was then and now it's today
I can't get up yet and so I'm here to stay
'Till someone comes along and takes my place
With a different name and, yes, a different face

You feelin' alright?
I'm not feelin' too good myself
You feelin' alright?
I'm not feelin' too good myself

CHAPTER FIVE

Feelin' Alright?

Why would I leave a band that was having so much success? That was on the acme of international acclaim?

I have thought about it many times over the years, and I always come back to the same conclusion: I wanted to make music without the trappings of stardom. I know this sounds crazy, but I simply wasn't ready for all the attention. I was a reluctant star.

So, I left Traffic. As I mentioned earlier, I just up and quit. I've thought about this so much since then. Since we had only played a bit and the album was not even out yet, I guess it was the anticipation of what was to come that felt potentially crushing. Also, I think I had a bit of what today is called "imposter syndrome." Did I really deserve what was about to happen? Was I the real deal? I was so young, and I just don't think I was ready for the big time.

As far as how the tabloids reacted, you would have thought I'd taken a shot at the Queen. My resignation made center page in the *News of the World,* one of the largest Sunday papers in all of England. It was a major story, which, ironically, was exactly what I was trying to escape. The guys in the band obviously weren't too happy about any of this, but they pulled it together as a trio and went off to tour America to promote *Dear Mr. Fantasy.* Weirdly, I was removed from the album cover in the States even though I wrote half of the material, including the band's biggest hit up to that point.

I stayed busy after my departure from Traffic. I produced an album for what could only be categorized as an extremely alternative band called Family. Family was managed by John Gilbert, son of a famous filmmaker from the 1930s. The band was one of the first examples of what came to be known as "progressive rock," meaning that it was experimental and unorthodox. This was also true about the studio tricks employed while making their album. This was before computers were part of the recording process, so we had to innovate. We were still working on four-track analog tape, so we created delay echo sounds by running long pieces of tape from the two-track recording machine around a desk and outstretched to a pencil. With more tape, there was more delay. I forget what the exact reason was, but Jimmy Miller stepped in about two-thirds into finishing the project. The album was released under the title *Music in a Doll's House*. The Beatles had originally intended to use the title *The Doll's House* for the double album they were recording during 1968, but when the Family album came out, that prompted The Beatles to go with the more minimalist title *The Beatles*—what is now commonly referred to as the White Album due to its plain white sleeve.

During this same period, the group Cream disbanded. I had developed a relationship with their drummer, Ginger Baker, who approached me about starting a new group. Bobby Gas, a great bass player and singer Ginger knew, joined us to form a trio. The band was to be called Salt in reference to the strategic arms talks that were taking place at the time.

We did a few rehearsals. Though it was an exciting and intriguing project, the three of us concluded that, compared to Cream, we weren't in the same game. On top of that, for me, nothing was quite jelling like it did with Traffic.

It may be a cliché, but life goes on—and, with the angels on our side, in some of the most serendipitous ways. In January 1968, I got to record with a genuinely brilliant musician—indeed, one of the greatest musicians of all time.

In London then, there were a number of private clubs that artists, musicians, actors, and "society people" would go to: The Bag O Nails, Blaze, and the Scotch of St. James were the main ones. There was always some live music. One night, at the Scotch of St. James, I was having a drink, listening to the band, when this guy gets up on stage to sit in. Tall and skinny, Levi's jacket and jeans, a big afro, and a white fender Stratocaster. By the time he'd finished playing a couple songs with the band, I thought that perhaps I should either give up playing guitar altogether or start to get a whole lot more serious about it. I mean this guy was just sitting in, but he was amazing, playing the guitar behind his head, with his teeth. Where the hell did he come from? The man was a gamechanger, an absolute renegade. (Then and now.) It wasn't until some time later, after Jimi Hendrix made his first recording, "Hey Joe," that I got to sit down with him in Blazes one evening. I, of course, was a huge fan. It turned out Jimi was a big fan of Traffic as well.

This sparked a relationship that led to many evenings spent together just listening to records and getting up in clubs and jamming together. One afternoon, we went to Jimi's friend's apartment after she'd gotten an advance copy of Bob Dylan's *John Wesley Harding*. We arrived to find a small gathering of people, including a band called The Pretty Things. Everybody was high on something, including a couple of people who were tripping on LSD, but Jimi and I were just intently listening to the music as if nobody else was in the room.

A few days later, I got a call from Jimi to meet him at Olympic Studios. "I'm going to do 'All Along the Watchtower,'" he told me.

When I arrived, Mitch Mitchell and Brian Jones were also there. Brian wasn't in the best of states, shall we say. Noel Redding wasn't there because, at the time, there was a rift between him and Hendrix. Jimi and

I had actually been talking about me joining his band, The Experience, as the bass player, even though it wasn't my main instrument. The session got set up with Mitch on drums, while Jimi and I sat facing one another and sharing a mic. I had an acoustic twelve-string, and Jimi had an acoustic six-string. That's how the basic track was recorded. The intro to "Watchtower" took me forever to get, maybe like eleven takes. I couldn't get the timing Jimi had. You'd expect him to say, "Hey, let me just do this," but instead, he had the patience with me to work it out.

I was there the whole session, watching Jimi put on the bass guitar part, and then all that electric guitar work on the track. Watching him work has to be one of the most inspiring musical experiences of my life. Jimi did his solo guitar work, and what really impressed me was the slide part that is on that record. He did it by putting his Strat on his lap and pulling out a Ronson cigarette lighter, which he used as a slide.

Brian Jones finally got up and added some percussion to the track. Jimi did his vocal parts and pretty much finished that song in one session other than mixing.

Watching him in the studio, it reminded me how many times I had tried to get him up to the cottage to jam with Traffic. But nobody in the band seemed interested when I brought up the idea. So, he never came up and played with us. How could you not make room for Jimi Hendrix? The way I had seen Traffic was almost like what Crosby, Stills, Nash, and Young would soon develop. That was your band, but you could also go off and do solo projects and play with other people. Then come back to the band. I imagined Traffic as a much more open musical situation where it would be great to have someone like Jimi stop by and play. Or Clapton. Or Jimmy Page. Or Jeff Beck. Whoever felt like it. Why not have a band that could be so flexible and could do anything including solo projects and side projects? Watching Jimi reminded me that perhaps my vision of Traffic was distinctly different from that of the other three members.

At a different session shortly thereafter, I finished up working on some other tracks with Jimi on which I played bass and sitar. To this day, I don't know what happened to those recordings. Maybe they will appear in the archives someday. Or maybe they're already out there, and I just don't know about them. I'd eventually also sing on "Crosstown Traffic," which of course *did* come out.

Except for the way he dressed, Jimi's stage persona was different than what he was like in person. He dressed like he was on stage all the time, but in private times, he was quiet. In the studio, he was all business. One of

his favorite guitar players, someone I also loved, was Albert King. There are a lot of superb guitar players out there, but there are no more Jimi Hendrixes in the world. Like The Beatles, Jimi was tremendously innovative in the studio. He used the studio like an instrument, always searching for new sounds and effects. My time with him was unforgettable.

Even now, Hendrix continues to inspire my playing. When I was with him, I was well aware that I was seeing history being made before my eyes. Being around that kind of creativity further compelled this kid from Worcester, England, to forge ahead in the unknown, uncharted territory of the world of rock and roll.

Hendrix and I developed a close friendship. While it didn't last for a long period of time, it was intense and powerful. Being with Hendrix, and hanging out with The Beatles, gave me permission to believe that I could do anything, that in the studio there were no rules, and that there was no greater freedom than music. These relationships galvanized me to be a better guitar player, to be a better songwriter, to be a better singer, and even to be a better person. It taught me, in no uncertain terms, that being authentic takes courage.

And one *must* be authentic to make great music. Those experiences reaffirmed that music was my life's path, so I pushed myself harder. While it was still difficult to endure the criticism of my old Traffic bandmates, I also knew that wasn't the end of the story. Not by a long shot.

Soon after recording "All Along the Watchtower" with Jimi, I took off with a knapsack and a guitar to a little Greek island called Hydra. Leonard Cohen had a house there, and the classic film *Phedra* was made there. I didn't have a lot of money, so I rented a room in a small boarding house near the little harbor. I basically lived on anise bread, retsina wine, fish, and feta cheese.

One late afternoon, I was sitting with some locals in an outdoor café beside the harbor when a man turned up with dead swallows tucked in his shirt. You could plainly see them since his shirt was half open. After he left, I asked, "What's the deal with the guy with the swallows?" They all said he was a little crazy. He would go way up to the mountaintop with a fishing line and a fly hook on the end of it, and let the wind carry the fly hook to catch swallows. I've seen some strange things in my day, but that memory in Hydra has to be one of the oddest.

I'd made the trip to the island because I had wanted to write songs that were 180 degrees different from "Hole in My Shoe"—songs that were timeless and more emotionally accessible. Since I was still trying to get over an unrequited love affair and was in a somewhat emotionally precarious state myself, I poured those feelings into some new songs.

One of them, "Feelin' Alright?," was based on my breakup with a girl named Linda Keith. She was a model for *Vogue* and was into traditional blues music. She turned me on to a lot of people, like John Lee Hooker, Muddy Waters, Elmore James, and others. She was also involved with Brian Jones and Jimi Hendrix. There is much myth and legend surrounding Linda Keith, even today. It's my understanding that, according to Keith Richards, she was the subject of the Stones classic "Ruby Tuesday." Someone said that Hendrix may also have written the song "Red House" about her. She was one of those people who was a cultural lightning rod. I fell for her and in a big way. Who wouldn't? I loved being with her, like everyone else. We'd met in a club or someplace, fell in

together, and I simply could not have her for myself as I desired.

Musically, "Feelin' Alright?" was an exercise in trying to write the simplest thing I could come up with. I'd been playing sitar for a while, which I used for "Hole in My Shoe," "Paper Sun," and the things I'd done with Hendrix, so that got me thinking about writing something very basic. There are only two chords in "Feelin' Alright?" It's simple. It's soulful while getting right to the point. A lot of people miss the nuance of the question mark in the title. The song's really about not feeling too good about myself. I was heartbroken at the time. I'd truly loved Linda, but she was so entwined with Brian Jones and Hendrix and others—so much so, she had no real place for me. I was young; she was experienced and worldly. My emotions could not handle it.

Over time, I ran out of money and had no ticket to get back to England. I made a collect phone call to Island Records since I was still signed with them to ask if they would buy me a plane ticket. I caught the ferry back to Athens to catch the flight the next day. Sitting in an outdoor café, I wrote the lyrics to "All Join In," with an idea of how it would go in my head. I caught my early morning flight, lyrics to new songs in hand, thus successfully ending my sojourn in Greece.

Not long after returning to London, I had enough Island Records royalties to get me to the United States where, coincidentally, I ended up in New York, where Traffic was working on their second album at the Record Plant. I went by the session despite knowing things might be awkward, to say the least. I had, after all, left the band. But they were cool;

we were all happy to see each other. We soon turned to talking music, and at that time they only had five songs, which isn't enough to finish an album.

"Well, I've got five new songs," I offered.

And so, through the music, Traffic was reunited. I'd taken my time off to think and to work on my songwriting and to evaluate what Traffic meant to me. I was more than ready. We returned to London to record my new songs, as well as play some shows. I was content to be back, and the guys all seemed to be pleased too. I'd grown up a bit and, as for the band, we'd put our differences aside. It was some of the best times in Traffic since our cottage days.

Takin' the Time to Find

I'm takin' the time to find some new roads into my mind
Discovering things and giving them wings
It's time that this boy learned to fly

How come I lose in love, every time I try?
How come I lose in love, but I just don't know why?
It seems I'm the first and the last to know
Don't think that it has to be so, don't think that it has to be so

Just when I think that I've found a reason for settling down
I still get the call, I'm missing it all, those changes are still coming down

How come I lose in love, every time I try?
How come I lose in love, but I just don't know why?
It seems I'm the first and the last to know
Don't think that it has to be so, don't think that it has to be so
I'm taking the time to find
I'm taking the time to find
I'm taking the time to find
I'm taking the time to find

CHAPTER SIX

Takin' the Time to Find

The album was already done, and we were getting ready to go out on tour to support the new album. This is when the meeting occurred at Chris Blackwell's house, and I was summarily fired.

Ego is such a weird thing. It's destroyed bands, marriages, friendships, families, and even countries. Once again, songs I had written for the band were picked for single releases ("Feelin' Alright?," "You Can All Join In") and appeared as if they were going to be hit singles, at that. We had all fallen back together for the simple reason that they needed some songs, and I had them in my back pocket. It wasn't like we sat down and had this huge, hyper-serious meeting. I felt I had grown over the course of the previous year and was more than ready for what was about to happen with Traffic. I was maturing. I had played with people like Hendrix, so I was feeling more confident. I definitely felt like my songwriting was improving.

But the band was still primarily about Steve Winwood. There's no denying that. He was a bona fide star, and despite the fact that we were kind of an artsy progressive band on paper, there were things about me I believe upset him.

For one, there was the perception that I was bringing "finished" songs to the table, rather than making them part of the group dynamic. In reality, they were just written on paper. I was totally open to how the others wanted to interpret those songs.

But perception trumped reality. Jim and Chris fell in line behind Steve. There was no mistaking that. And I think Steve decided that perhaps the abilities I was bringing into the band were maybe a bit of a threat to him. He's never told me that; that's just my feeling. It does not take away from the fact that I still think he is an absolute genius and someone I will always admire and be a fan of. But I think, at that moment in time, my capacities, my skills—even, hell, my *bravery*—may have gotten in the way of his vision of the band. While I was thoroughly hurt and disappointed about the final breakup of Traffic, the situation provided some serious fodder for soul searching.

My spirit was somewhat picked up by a phone call from Chris Blackwell's friend Denny Cordell, who was managing and producing a new artist named Joe Cocker. Denny told me he had recorded a song with Joe—one that I had written and sung on the second Traffic album—and asked if I would like to hear it.

Sometimes the author is not the best interpreter of their own work. From the opening piano played by Artie Butler to Joe's very soulful and distinctive voice, the song went from "Feelin' Alright?" (with a question mark) to "Feeling Alright." As I mentioned, when I wrote the song, "Feelin' Alright?" was a question, and my answer emphasized "not feeling too good myself." Cocker's interpretation was optimistic and upbeat. I loved it and was blown away by what Joe had done with my song. Cocker liked the song so much he chose it as the lead track on his 1969 debut album *With A Little Help From My Friends*. His version of "Feeling Alright" charted at number 69 on the US singles chart, and his 1972 rerelease charted at number 33. Traffic's version, by contrast, didn't break the top 100 even though it was an audience favorite.

I love hearing other artists' interpretations of my songs. I don't feel a sense of ownership in that way; rather, I support and embrace creativity. "Feelin' Alright?" has been covered by more than fifty recording artists and, at some time or another, has been played by every bar band. And it's still being played to this day. Joe Cocker's "Feeling Alright," for me, is the definitive version. It still sounds as good today as it did in 1969.

Over the years I had the chance to share the stage with Joe doing my song. I consider Joe to be one of my angels, and I owe him a debt of gratitude. Who knew that simple two-chord song would take on such a life of its own? At the time, of course, I didn't know any of this would happen. I was making my way the best I could, which is to say I was in a headspace of uncertainty.

What to do now? What I did know was that I wanted to stay in music; of that I was clear. Should I look for another band or strike out on my own? I felt I'd exhausted my options in England. I felt stale and uninspired . . . until I opened up to the idea of going to America again. Now that felt bold. I was ready to leave my home and move to the place of the origins of it all—rock and roll, jazz, blues, R&B, and gospel.

I had royalties and tour money, enough to get myself to Los Angeles, and with a single suitcase, an acoustic guitar, and a lot of ambition, I was LA-bound.

Just a month or two after I was fired from Traffic, Steve Winwood quit the band. That should have effectively killed the group, but Chris Blackwell wasn't quite finished with the idea yet. Even though I was just settling into life in Los Angeles, Chris rang me up and offered to fly me back to London. Soon I was back in England and reunited with two of my former bandmates, Jim Capaldi and Chris Wood. We created a new band at Blackwell's behest and soon added a keyboard player and singer, Wynder K. Frog, to fill Winwood's role.

We began playing concerts under the name Mason, Capaldi, Wood & Frog, with an emphasis on songs from Traffic, as well as new songs I'd written. The band was well received, as we were widely seen as Traffic reborn, only with a fresh name. We even got to open for Hendrix at the Royal Albert Hall, where Chris and I got up and jammed with Hendrix during his performance.

In deference to Frog's playing, however, it wasn't the same without Winwood. His talent was too unique to replace. We called it quits after three months. With even more conviction than before, I left England once again and returned to Los Angeles to stay.

I didn't know many people when I landed back in Los Angeles, and far fewer knew me. My sister, who admittedly I knew very little, was in San Diego, but I opted to stay in LA. This was LA in 1969—hippies were still dancing in the street on Sunset Boulevard outside the Whisky a Go Go. It was all about good times and good songs.

Fortunately, my new friend Gram Parsons took me in. I first got to know Gram at Olympic Studios in London. He had been playing with The Byrds, who had gone on to South Africa to perform. He didn't want to go, so he was hanging out with The Rolling Stones while they were working on *Beggars Banquet*. Gram and I became friends during those sessions when I joined them for "Street Fighting Man." Once I arrived back in the States, I slept on Gram's couch for a while until I got my bearings. One of the first places we went to hang out was at the home of Cass Elliot, aka Mama Cass of The Mamas & the Papas. She lived up on Woodstock Road in Laurel Canyon. I liked her immediately. I found her to be kind of like the old vaudeville legend Sophie Tucker—acerbic, sharp, funny, and a very talented singer.

Coincidentally, at our time of meeting, Cass had two friends of mine from England living at her house, the actor Ben Carruthers (*Ship of Fools, The Dirty Dozen*) and his wife. I automatically felt like I had kindred spirits up in Laurel Canyon. Eventually, I left Gram's and moved into the Chateau Marmont, where I'd write songs, but I still continued visiting Cass's house, which swiftly became my home away from home. Lots of colorful characters were always coming in and out of her place. Cass knew someone from Wham-O, the toy company, so we got to test out and play with early versions of whatever they were marketing. I became a proficient Frisbee player. One of the more interesting things they brought for us to play with was a serious blowgun. And I do mean serious. You could kill people with this thing. It was about six feet long with five-inch metal darts and damn accurate. Fortunately, that's one "toy" that never made it to the mass market. We sure had fun with them all up there, though.

Other people who frequented the house were Amy Folger (heir to the Folger coffee fortune) and her boyfriend, Voytek Frykowski. One evening we all went to visit the beautiful actress Sharon Tate at the rustic yet elegant home she shared with film director Roman Polanski off Benedict Canyon on Cielo Drive.

Tate was good friends with Folger. It was one of my first glimpses into the Hollywood scene, up there in that house perched high up on the side of a mountain, with the city lights of Los Angeles far off in the distance, glittering like marquees in the night—like gold.

Plus, there was so much great music and so many talented musicians up at Cass's place all the time—who could stay away? David Crosby, Stephen Stills, Graham Nash, and Joni Mitchell—people who would ultimately become veritable gods in rock and roll.

But this era wasn't all as light and airy as it's been mythologized. There were darker characters who frequented Cass's place, including two shady types named Billy Doyle and Charles Tacot. My entanglement with them eventually messed up my life on many levels, including my music rights and some serious money issues. But we'll get to that.

While living in sunny California was radically different than the London scene, I took to it. It fit like a glove. The "California Sound" was being birthed all around me, and I was absorbing the flavor of it all. I was young and far away from home, but it forced me to grow up, show up, and make a stand in my own music, which included playing and recording with many of the folks I'd met at Cass's house, including Crosby, Stills, and Nash. I worked on my music every damn day. My own sound started taking shape; I could feel it. Good fortune shined on me often, and, thankfully, I had the goods to back it all up when the moments arrived.

I was writing music but still hadn't sorted out what to do about a band. One night, Gram took me out to a country music club in the San Fernando Valley called The Palomino. "There's a band I want you to hear," he told me, referring to Delaney & Bonnie and Friends.

I was already aware of them, but seeing them live brought an entirely new level of appreciation. They absolutely blew me away with their stage presence and talent. Delaney was a dark, brooding Mississippian whose bluesy, soulful guitar playing and singing blended perfectly with his band partner and wife, Bonnie. I mean, her voice

could move a mountain. Together, with Bobby Whitlock, there was vocal wizardry at work.

I sat in with them that night and absolutely loved it. I felt right at home, musically as well as with their personalities. It was fun, of course, but there was also an earnestness and authenticity about what they were doing. I felt I was getting closer to the roots of the music that drew me to America. The Palomino became a somewhat regular hang out. I went one night to see Jerry Lee Lewis and found myself in the company of a few celebs that had the same idea. You never knew who you might run into at the Palomino.

I casually dropped in to play a few more times with Delaney & Bonnie. One night, at the bar after their set, Delaney invited me to join the band for their upcoming summer tour. I liked the sound of that. I wanted to be in a band again, but not just any band. *This* band.

By that point, Eric Clapton had formed yet another supergroup after Cream with none other than my old bandmates Steve Winwood, Ginger Baker, and Ric Grech. Wasn't that a twist of fate? Winwood fired me and, in less than a month, he had quit Traffic to form Blind Faith with Clapton. Winwood and Clapton were an excellent combination, and I was excited to hear what they were doing live. One of the best singers and one of the best guitar players together seemed like the ideal pairing.

As destiny would have it, we would all be together again, on the same

bill, albeit in two different bands because Clapton loved the idea of bringing Delaney & Bonnie out on the road with Blind Faith.

Before we set out, however, we did our own short tour of the States to get ready. And ready we would be! Playing in Delaney & Bonnie's group renewed my faith in what being in a band is all about.

During this time, The Rolling Stones were in Los Angeles recording their album *Let It Bleed*. They were aware of the buzz about Delaney & Bonnie, and a couple of years later they would have our sax player Bobby Keys playing with them. Before we hit the road on tour, the Stones wanted Bonnie to sing a duet with Mick on the song "Gimme Shelter." Delaney thought it was a great idea—until he didn't. As Bonnie explained to me later, once Delaney started drinking, he got jealous, went to the recording session, and yanked Bonnie right out of the booth. She'd already worked out her part and recorded it, but the Stones brought in Merry Clayton to track what Bonnie had already laid down. And the rest is rock and roll history.

An old bus was procured and off we went, Delaney & Bonnie and Friends. Now, this was before the days of luxury touring buses. This was a bare-bones Greyhound with little more than the seats and some space in the back to pack our gear. But we didn't need much. There wouldn't be much sleeping on this particular bus (or anywhere on the tour for that matter), but there would

be lots of playing, lots of singing, lots of laughing, and lots of drinking and drugs.

This is how I first saw the United States, driving from show to show. And what a band it was, including Bobby, Rita Coolidge, Jim Gordon, Carl Radle, Jim Price, and Bobby Whitlock. Looking back on it, it's hard to believe the amount of talent that was crammed onto that old bus. My decision to move to America was turning out to be even better than I had hoped for.

We were warmed up, to be sure, by the time

we joined up with Blind Faith. We met them in Connecticut, and it was weird when I first saw Winwood—and that's putting it mildly.

It was at a hotel, not on stage. He offered no eye contact, no nothing. I thought it was strange behavior. I mean, I was standing *right* there. He had been my pal and bandmate, someone with whom I'd created unforgettable memories of jamming in a dilapidated cottage in the wilderness before we hit number two with our first hit. Now he was aloof and thoroughly disengaged.

Clapton, on the other hand, was quite different. He was down-to-earth and approachable. We had our old bus, while Blind Faith was traveling by private jet. There was no doubt about who was opening for whom, but the music was awesome, and that is, in the end, all that mattered.

Our first official gig with Blind Faith was at the newly opened Madison Square Garden in New York City. If anybody told me that, just a few months after being fired from Traffic, I would be on the same bill with Steve Winwood in New York at the Garden, I wouldn't have believed them. But in rock and roll—and especially in life—I was fast learning not to get too comfortable in any situation. Things can and will change

quickly and unpredictably.

Madison Square Garden was a sold-out show with 20,000 fans. There was a huge demand for Blind Faith, certainly, but the place was packed early when we took the stage for our opening set.

Just as we started our first song, the power on stage blew out. Delaney and I grabbed our acoustic guitars as 20,000 people became silent, their full attention on every note while we sang and played without any power. Once the power kicked back on, we plugged in and forgot about it. We *rocked* the Garden.

I wish I could have said the same for Blind Faith. Night after night, it seemed Delaney & Bonnie got all the raves from both the audiences and the press. While there was huge talent (and bigger names) in Blind Faith, you just couldn't get around the dynamic energy of Delaney & Bonnie. That band could stand up to anything. The music of Delaney & Bonnie was soulful, funky, and kicked ass. They—we—nailed it.

As the tour progressed, Clapton started hanging out with us. He seemed to be as much a part of our band as he was Blind Faith. I honestly can't imagine what musician would not have wanted to hang out with a group like that. He traveled on our modest tour bus rather than the fancy private jet. He would even join us on stage from time to time. Clapton's relationship with Delaney would play a very important role in Eric's future, influencing his songwriting and singing, all the way up to Delaney producing the self-titled *Eric Clapton* album.

**Backstage on the Delaney & Bonnie tour with George Harrison (L)
and Eric Clapton (R). Trumpeter Jim Price is in the background.**

Eric was at an interesting point in his life at that time. He had been deified for years, with "Clapton is God" emblazoned all over London after first getting spraypainted on the wall of the Islington underground station. But he was looking for something different, and I understood that. Being held on a pedestal isn't what it seems—not that I compared myself to his stature, but I'd had enough of a taste of it. I empathized that he just wanted to be a guy in a band. I had never spent much time one-on-one with Clapton before then, but when he was with us on the bus, he was humble and unassuming—and, without a doubt, an exceptional guitar player. I liked him because he seemed to hold it all in perspective. I admired that he didn't buy into the hype. It can be intoxicating, and if anyone deserved to believe his own press, it was Clapton. But he was, and still is, the real thing.

While on tour one night, I was in the hotel bar having a drink, when the evening news came on and reported the Manson murders. It hit a little too close to home, literally and figuratively, since I lived close to the site and was friends with two of the victims, Abby Folger and Voytek Frykowski. I'd had dinner with them. I'd gotten high with them. I'd met Sharon Tate. It seemed the era of peace and love, that glorious hippie freedom and togetherness, was coming to a close. It struck a chord with us all.

But the show must go on—and I mean that both literally and figuratively.

In addition to Madison Square Garden, the Forum in Los Angeles was the other notably prestigious venue we played. Relatively new at the time, these two arenas would soon become the gold standard for successful rock bands. In 1969, when we were there, neither place had hosted much in the way of music. We arrived at the Forum on August 15. Some 3,000 miles or so east, in a pasture in upstate New York, the Woodstock festival was getting underway that very same day. Jimi Hendrix would be blowing minds there in a couple of days. Crosby, Stills, Nash & Young would be playing the first big show of their career as a band. National music history was being made. But at the Forum, it was the usual backstage scene with industry suits, beautiful women, and all stratum of musicians.

There was also an unfamiliar strangeness in the air. The Manson murders had taken place just a week or so earlier, so the customary casual vibe of the city wasn't palpable, wasn't present. Backstage was buzzing. You could hear people whispering about it. Everybody knew someone who knew someone associated with the tragedy, including me.

We always were able to set our troubles aside and put on a hell of a show. The *Los Angeles Times* wrote a day later, "Delaney & Bonnie and Friends were stunning, with an exuberantly pitched set of the lovely gospel-country-R 'n' B for which they are becoming internationally famous." I'd found my second home away from home.

I noticed her as I was walking toward our limo after the gig. We had briefly caught one another's eyes earlier in the evening before I played.

But now she was part of the small crowd collected to get a glimpse of whatever "star" might happen to pass by the tunnel where tour buses entered to get bands safely inside the venue. She was beautiful. I remember the vision like it was yesterday: her brown halter top, matching slacks, and sky-high heels that made her taller than six feet. I was with David Anderle from A&M records, and I said to him, "Wow, who the fuck is that? I'm gonna marry her."

He smiled. "That's Lorraine," he said knowingly.

David introduced us, and there was definitely a mutual attraction. I didn't know she was a groupie. I didn't know she had already been with Jimi Hendrix and many others. I'm not sure it would've mattered, frankly. Groupies back in the late 1960s and early 1970s were an unofficial part of the music business. I took her number and left Lorraine that night with the promise of being in touch as soon as I got back to Los Angeles after the tour.

From LA, we went and played in Santa Barbara, Houston, San Antonio, Salt Lake City, and finally, Phoenix, where the police were particularly hostile toward our long hair and drug-taking reputations—none of which was unfounded. But in those days, some felt we were actually dangerous. When Clapton tried to join us to play some tambourine, the cops violently yanked him off stage. He was furious. Then Bonnie fell off the stage, ten feet onto concrete, and all hell broke loose. The cops dragged her into an office and would not let us near her. Fists were almost thrown, but eventually, we managed to get in there. Delaney carried her out on his shoulder.

Blind Faith went on to play one more show, in Honolulu, but without us. That was the end of the tour and the end of Blind Faith, too. It was a successful tour for us, but it wasn't over yet. Delaney & Bonnie were booked to travel throughout England and Europe later in the year. And I was all in.

One of the more notable shows that we did in Europe was at Croyden's Fairfield Hall. Eric came to the show and brought George Harrison with him. Delaney and I, of course, were all over Eric to sit in, and also George. George looked at me and said, "But I don't know any of these songs."

One of the songs I had recorded with Delaney & Bonnie was called "Comin' Home." I had played a simple recurring slide guitar part for the solo, actually replacing the solo Eric Clapton had laid down after Delaney called me late one night to say he didn't like it. George wasn't too familiar with playing slide guitar, but with a little rehearsal in the dressing room, I taught him the part.

He joined us, along with Eric, on stage for that song. It's funny how things that seem to be throw-away moments turn out to have big ramifications. It wasn't until many years later that I read an interview with George where he related the story of me teaching him this part and how it became the inspiration for him to start playing that trademark slide guitar that he used on so many recordings.

The rest of the tour was a marvelous journey. In Germany, the fans were really pissed off because Eric Clapton was advertised but not part of the show. Things got much better once we got the promoters to redo the posters. At the tour's end, John Lennon had us all come down to play at his "Peace for Christmas" concert at the Lyceum. Later, I joined George Harrison in his studio along with many other great artists and players to work on his acclaimed album *All Things Must Pass*.

Unlike an experience playing one-on-one in the studio with Jimi Hendrix, this was a much more sprawling affair that left me with very few specific memories. I mean, the room was always packed. Many of the players were people I was highly familiar with from Delaney & Bonnie and other experiences, including Bobby Whitlock, Eric Clapton, Carl Radle, Jim Gordon, Jim Price, and others. Then you had Ringo Starr, Billy Preston, and many other legends. My guitar playing ended up on several songs, including "Beware of Darkness," "I Dig Love," and "Thanks for the Pepperoni." George was so busy organizing and arranging and overseeing the sessions with Phil Spector that we really didn't hang out, but I was very happy for him once the record was released. It obviously includes some of his most well-known songs, including "My Sweet Lord" and "What Is Life." For a guy who had only typically contributed about two songs per Beatles album, George let the world know what he was capable of. The album stands today as one of the most acclaimed of that era.

Next, I found myself camped out at Eric Clapton's house as a new member of Derek and the Dominos. Eric had hijacked what was essentially the entire Delaney & Bonnie band, and for good reason. I don't begrudge him that. His home in Surrey was a striking, Moorish-style mansion, and we all set up there, living together, similar to Traffic's cottage days.

Bobby Whitlock, Eric Clapton, and me onstage at the one show I played as a member of Derek and the Dominoes.

This was something that, for me, potentially had all that Traffic had and more. We started working on new material, which we went into the studio and recorded, and we also did one live show in London.

Unfortunately, this is when Eric started getting into heroin, courtesy of drummer Jim Gordon. Not a lot was getting done. I grew bored and frustrated with all the dead time. Meanwhile, I was having my own issues with cocaine.

Looking back, I would have loved to have been a part of that band for longer, but it was not meant to be. Derek and the Dominoes went on to make one of the most seminal albums of all time, *Layla and Other Assorted Love Songs*. Instead, I went back to LA to make a solo record, *Alone Together.* "I think he has a fantastic touch," Eric said of me in a *Rolling Stone* interview soon after I departed. "I love the way he plays guitar. And his songs are great. But as yet we're two different personalities, and the music that comes out of those personalities at this time is quite different. And he has a lot of things on his plate at the moment that he's trying to get together. He should go out to America, and do a tour in his own name. . . . until he's really got some kind of recognition he deserves as a solo artist."

Eric Clapton talking with me backstage.

When I got back to Los Angeles, I reconnected with Lorraine, whom I'd met that night at the Forum. She wanted to take me to Big Sur. I had heard how beautiful it was driving up Highway One along the Pacific Coast, and the Big Sur Music Festival was happening at the Esalen Institute, a retreat center that focused on humanistic alternative education.

About 15,000 people camped out for three miles up and down Highway One for the two-day festival, which included Joni Mitchell, Joan Baez, and Crosby, Stills, Nash & Young, among others. The bands were set up on one side of the swimming pool, with a breathtaking view of the Pacific Ocean behind us. A documentary film was made of the festival.

Though I wasn't formally on the bill, I got to perform a couple of songs with CSNY. I knew Graham from the Hollies and had become friends with Stephen Stills, so I was invited to sit in, though I hadn't expected it. It was spontaneous and the first-ever live performances of my songs "Only You Know and I Know" and "World in Changes."

After the festival, Lorraine and I went to a hotel in Carmel, which was even more quiet, charming, and low key back in 1969 than it still is now.

When we drove back to Los Angeles, neither of us was aware that our son True had just been conceived.

Bonnie Bramlett is an American singer, along with her husband Delaney, of the acclaimed and beloved band Delaney & Bonnie. She is a one-time musical partner who performed and toured together with Dave and is also a friend.

Bonnie Bramlett:

I first met Dave when he played with us at the Palomino. We'd all heard that he had been fired from Traffic. Who would fire this guy? He was so crazy talented and such a soulful guitar player. We just loved him right away and made him part of our band. I really didn't know many white artists at that time. I was a blues singer from East St. Louis. I was hardcore. But now I'm hearing about guys like Dave and Eric Clapton and George Harrison, and my eyes are getting opened.

And then we hit the road! We just had a raggedy old Greyhound bus, no couches or card tables. We played a lot of music on the bus and did a lot of cocaine. But we went out there like tornadoes. Every show we played, we made sure everybody knew who we were when we left. After playing for a couple of months, we did the tour with Blind Faith. My opinion? Great musicians. I get it and all of that. But I just thought the music was boring. I loved the fact that Eric Clapton wanted to hang out with us. Me and Rita Coolidge just loved him.

What I loved about Dave was that he was a calming influence on Delaney. Delaney could get really nervous before shows and get a little crazy. But Dave was just so cool, and that had a real effect on Delaney.

I think my best memory is when we played Madison Square Garden. This was a big show. So exciting. So we go out there, and we're about to start playing our first number, "Poor Elijah." And the power goes out! The packed house, 20,000 people, and no power. Well, I watched Dave and Delaney. Both of them just grabbed acoustic guitars, and then me and Bobby Whitlock and Rita got behind them and we did the first couple of numbers acoustically. The audience at the Garden seemed to sense what was going on, and they got so quiet you could hear a pin drop. Had Dave and Delaney lost their cool in that moment, it would've been a disaster. But they just had this unspoken thing between them. Then the power came back on, and we blew the roof off of that place.

From there, Dave came with us over to Europe and was an important part of the band. And I mean, without "Only You Know and I Know," I'm not sure we would be talking about Delaney & Bonnie that much today. That became such an important part of our repertoire, and we have Dave to thank for that. I know when he just arrived in America, he wasn't sure what he was going to do, but I'm so glad he connected with us. I think we helped him a little bit, and he certainly helped us.

World in Changes

Things could be lazy if they weren't so crazy
And I wasn't following you
Running in circles, won't find me no purpose
It's right here with you and what I do

Changes of season are nearly as pleasing
As watching the changes in you
Turn for a new day in search of a new way
But are you sure that it will do

World in changes, still going through
I've got a lot to learn about you
World in changes, still going through
You've got a lot to learn about me too
You've got a lot to learn about me too

I said, well, now let's see what you really mean to me
I'll tell the truth cause I can't pretend
Oh, find yourself a real friend and then you've nearly reached the end
Of all of this runnin' round we do

World in changes, still going through
I've got a lot to learn about you
World in changes, still going through
You've got a lot to learn about me too
You've got a lot to learn about me too

CHAPTER SEVEN

World in Changes

Alan Pariser arrived in Los Angeles in the mid-1960s and became a minor player within the burgeoning music scene. One of his first claims to fame was coproducing a benefit concert headlined by a new LA band called The Doors. Pariser had also attended the 1966 Monterey Jazz Festival at the Monterey Fairgrounds, which gave him an idea. Joining forces with a promoter friend named Ben Shapiro, the pair concocted the idea to produce a rock and roll festival at the same venue a year later. The Mamas & the Papas were big then, so the two reached out to bandleader John Phillips and the quartet's manager-producer, Lou Adler, who said they'd consider it.

Pariser and Shapiro's proposal came up during a later discussion with Adler again, and within twenty-four hours, the Monterey International Pop Festival had been conceived as a three-day nonprofit charitable event. With a scant six weeks to map it out and get it on its feet, Phillips and Adler feverishly started planning. Pariser became the festival coproducer and was a member of the board of governors that included Phillips, Adler, and Paul McCartney, plus Mick Jagger, Andrew Loog Oldham, Roger McGuinn, Terry Melcher, Donovan, Smokey Robinson, Johnny Rivers, and Brian Wilson.

So Pariser was making a name for himself. One night, in early 1968, he witnessed one of the first live performances by Delaney and Bonnie Bramlett and their new backing group, which they called "Friends" because the lineup was in constant flux. He became their manager, and once I started playing with the band, he became my manager as well.

By then, Pariser was also a partner in Group 3 Management and worked closely with famed photographer Barry Feinstein and designer Tom Wilkes. Their graphic design company, called Camouflage Productions, became the in-house art department for a new boutique label known as Blue Thumb Records. Blue Thumb had been started in 1968 by Bob Krasnow, along with Don Graham and Tommy LiPuma. Krasnow had been in the business since the 1950s when he started out working as a promotions guy for James Brown.

Some of the Blue Thumb Records staff, including Tommy Lipuma on the far right.

One of the first Blue Thumb artists was Captain Beefheart. "Blue Thumb" was actually the name Beefheart wanted to use for his backing band, but Krasnow didn't like the name for the group. He liked it for his label, so he adopted it. (Beefheart would call his group The Magic Band.) Blue Thumb's first notable releases after Beefheart were records by Ike & Tina Turner and Tyrannosaurus Rex (soon to be renamed T. Rex). Much later in life, Krasnow went on to become CEO of Warner Bros' Elektra/Asylum labels and a cofounder of the Rock & Roll Hall of Fame. But in the late 1960s, he was a young and hungry record executive.

In 1969, I was being courted by a number of major labels, but of my association with Pariser, I went with Blue Thumb. It was a boutique label, similar to Chris Blackwell's Island Records. Blackwell still retained publishing rights on all my songs from the band, including "Feelin' Alright?" C'est la vie.

I was occasionally hanging out with Crosby, Stills, and Nash at Peter Tork's house in Laurel Canyon, where they stashed themselves away from the world for rehearsals. Even though I knew Graham because we had toured Europe together back when he was in The Hollies and I was in Traffic, I gravitated toward Stills because he was the guitar player. Steven taught me a couple of interesting tunings, one of which, an F tuning, I used for my song "Only You Know and I Know." He and I cut an early version of it, which is something I wish I had a copy of today. Steven was and is a great and innovative guitar player. I just wish he'd kept the Jimi Hendrix solo on "Love the One You're With," which few people are aware actually existed! Supposedly, Stills didn't care for what Jimi played and opted for the organ solo instead. I never heard it myself but heard *about* it from reliable sources back then.

I wanted to make an album that would blend both acoustic and electric guitars. I knew the songs I'd been writing were good. I'd worked on them for over a two-year period, and my guitar playing was getting more fluid and articulate.

In the end, though, it was all about the songs. As the adage goes in the music business, "It's the song, the song, the song." Touring with Delaney & Bonnie and soaking up influences while traversing the country had shaped my writing in a new way. I had been exposed to many parts of the country, the South in particular, where so many American musical roots were planted. And so I was anxious to go and start recording the album.

Tommy LiPuma was coproducing with me at Sunset Sound Studios, and he spared little expense in recruiting some of the best session players of the era—including Leon Russell, Jim Keltner, Jim Gordon, John Simon, and most of the Delaney & Bonnie band. (Despite many rumors, Clapton was not there.) To be playing with this caliber of musicians on songs I had written was more than I could have ever hoped for. These people were there to play not only what I had written, but also to bring their own unique touches to each and every song. I knew then how amazing it was, and I sure know it now. We were very efficient in the studio because I knew the musicians, and I'd played with them all. Since I'd already written the songs (some of which I'd originally intended for the third Traffic album), all our time was spent on how to interpret them. I gave everyone freedom because I knew these guys had the right feel for the work.

Something interesting happened during the making of the record. Jim Capaldi had come over to visit me. One night we were hanging out, and I was looking through one of his lyric notebooks. I had put together the musical idea for the song that became one of my standards, "Look at You, Look at Me." But I didn't have any words for it. I had the chord sequence—that galloping, rhythmic sort of thing—but no lyrics. Then I saw these words he had written, and I thought to myself, "These are perfect, these will fit perfectly over the music I'm writing!" And that's how that song came together.

The recording was finished, and I was certainly proud of what we'd done. Whether people liked it or not, I had accomplished what I'd set out to do. But it wasn't completely done yet. The cover! I wanted something distinctive, even inimitable. We'd always been diligent with our covers in Traffic, so I got together with Barry Feinstein of Camouflage to come up with something innovative. I didn't want a conventional sleeve, so we came up with a jacket that folds out over several layers into a sunrise with the actual vinyl colored with a sunburst effect—a work of art that could then be hung on the wall. It was fancy. And yes, expensive, but I fought for it.

Barry Feinstein had the idea for shooting the actual cover. He picked me up one day, and we went over to Western Costume, the famous Hollywood warehouse that held millions of items for dress-up. We picked over capes and hats and shirts, and Barry finally settled on a top hat and drape coat. "I see you as Jiminy Cricket," he said. "You're like a musical conscience, and that's how I want you to come across on the album."

From there, we headed out to Joshua Tree, a moonscape desert several hours outside Los Angeles, not far from Palm Springs. Back then, Joshua Tree had yet to become a National Park. Its beauty was unmanicured, wild and rugged. Barry had done a lot of shooting out there already with other bands and artists, including Bob Dylan and Delaney & Bonnie. So there I was—in top hat, trousers, and dress coat—in ninety-five-degree weather. We were at the foot of a rock formation. Barry said, "Go climb

up there." I was about halfway up a good-sized hill when he called out, "Look out for rattlesnakes!" I promptly stopped, turned to the camera, and that's the album's shot right there.

At the pressing plant, colors were selected for the vinyl effect and, as the presses were rolling for *Alone Together,* pellets of different colors were dropped in by hand. There was no way to actually control how the colors mixed together, so every one of the albums came out differently—not necessarily what I envisioned but still unique, which is precisely what I wanted. Over the years, disc jockeys would tell me that the fact they could barely see the separation grooves on the vinyl meant that oftentimes, they would wind up playing the entire damned side of the record. Fine with me. That really helped promote it.

Right after *Alone Together* was released, Blue Thumb Records made plans for a somewhat elaborate promotion to call attention to the album. Delaney & Bonnie and Friends were playing at the Santa Monica Civic Auditorium. While I was no longer officially part of their band, we were all good friends, so I was set to open the show and then come out with them for a few songs after that. It was one of my earliest moments as a solo artist, and I was scared to death. Thankfully, Leon Russell would be accompanying me on piano. To make it special, Blue Thumb chartered a double-decker English bus to transport all the important music

journalists from Beverly Hills to the Civic Auditorium just in time for my set. They filled the bus with big baskets of food for the press, including potato salad, chicken, bread, and wine. Smart move, considering that most journalists love nothing more than free food and booze—except maybe some cocaine, which was probably provided as well.

During the leisurely ride to the venue, the Blue Thumb PR people were going to talk up the album (and me) in anticipation of the show. But then, as luck would have it, the bus died right in the middle of Pico Boulevard, nowhere near the Santa Monica Civic Auditorium. Another bus was summoned, which took a little while to arrive and, unfortunately, the journalists were rushed into the auditorium in time to catch my last number. My big solo debut, and the press didn't even get a chance to see it.

It was still OK. I had a great time playing with Delaney & Bonnie that night, and my solo set was very well received by the crowd—which is really what I cared more about than the journalists. Perhaps a slightly shaky way to start the press campaign for an album that the label was excited about, but we all managed to survive.

Advance orders in the United States for *Alone Together* were more than 100,000. The album was eventually certified Gold and became one of Blue Thumb's biggest hits ever.

This should have meant that the label would have valued me and not balked if I came to them looking for a renegotiation, right?

Well, not exactly. But that mess was still a couple of years away. I had my first solo record, it was garnering great reviews right out of the gate, and I should've been on my way to solo stardom.

Right?

Bruce Botnick is an acclaimed audio engineer and record producer. He was the engineer on *Alone Together*.

Bruce Botnick:
I had been doing lots of work for Tony LiPuma, and he told me he had signed Dave Mason. I was very excited about that. I was a huge fan of the first Traffic album, and I knew that Dave was both a talented

songwriter and performer. I was very anxious for those sessions to start. I was basically the recording engineer on all of those sessions. What stands out to me, first and foremost, was the quality of the songs that Dave brought in. One after another, you just realized that he had assembled an incredibly special collection of songs. Each one was different, and each one was special. And then on top of that, when you had players like Jim Keltner, Jim Gordon, Leon Russell, and all of those folks from Delaney & Bonnie, I mean, what more could you ask for? The quality of all of those players meant that the sessions were extremely professional. Everybody was there to work. There may have been a little drinking and cocaine going on, but nothing that prevented us from knocking down song after song and getting remarkably professional takes out of everybody. The sessions were just wonderful. I distinctly remember Dave and Leon Russell sitting off together, getting lost in deep discussions about American music. Then we would start recording and they would implement everything they had been talking about. These were true masters at work, all of them.

At a certain point, near the end of the sessions, I was called away to go work on The Doors album, LA Woman. My brother, who had been working as an assistant engineer on Dave's sessions, took over for me. The weeks went by, and I got a call from Tommy. He told me he needed some studio time because there were one or two other songs that needed to be cut, and Sunset Sound was booked. So I booked some time at Elektra and everybody came back and recorded what became Dave's first real solo hit, "Only You Know and I Know." A total classic right out of the gate. Dave just had this thing where he would go for performance and feel rather than perfection. He was great about that. Some guitar players I've worked with do the exact opposite. He knew what he wanted, but he always left room for the magic that happens in the best recording sessions. I still think he's one of the great and underrated guitar players of his generation.

Waitin' on You

My feelings have been deceived
Well, there's no one that I can believe, oh, no
It's all because I couldn't see
That the best friend that I'll have is me, yeah

But I'm just waitin' on you, hoping that you'll be here soon
Still waitin' to see if you really meant what you said to me
Waitin' on you, waitin' on, waitin' on you
Waitin' on you, waitin' on, waitin' on you
Waitin' on you

There's no need to play act for me
'Cause you grab what you can while it's free
Just come right out with what you mean
Are the roses as red as they seem?

But I'm just waitin' on you, hoping that you'll be here soon
Still waitin' to see if you really meant what you said to me
Waitin' on you, waitin' on, waitin' on you
Waitin' on you, waitin' on, waitin' on you
Waitin' on you

Thought that by now you'd have changed
But the name of your game's still the same
I ain't trying to say nothing new, no, no, no
Just to make you happy will more than you

But I'm still waitin' on you, hoping that you'll be here soon
Still waitin' to see if you really meant what you said to me
Waitin' on you, waitin' on you, waitin' on you
Waitin' on you, waitin' on you, waitin' on you
Waitin' on you

CHAPTER EIGHT

Waitin' on You

I like surprises, especially good ones. I embrace the unexpected. Musically, my tastes range from Bach to Elmore James, and as much as I love singing and playing the blues, I equally love melodic songs with lots of harmonies.

With that in mind, making music with Cass Elliot was not a huge stretch for me. There were many times at her house in Laurel Canyon when I would spontaneously pick up an acoustic guitar and we'd sing together. Making an album together just became a natural next step. She had already released two solo albums at that time, but she was looking for something more collaborative, so we released *Dave Mason & Cass Elliot* in March 1971. We had originally planned on having a third member named Ned Doheny be a part of this new arrangement, which I think would have been a great move. Ned came out of that Jackson Browne style. He was a really good singer and played guitar

really well. His family was very prominent (Doheny Drive is his family's namesake). Unfortunately, Ned didn't want to go on the road to support the music. I wrote five of the songs on the record and cowrote two of them with Cass. She was a great writing partner, so funny and witty on one hand yet profound and evocative on the other. Singing with her, our blending of vocals, was artistically gratifying.

Dave Mason & Cass Elliot made a little bit of noise. Because Cass was a prominent TV personality, it got us booked on everything from *The Tonight Show* to *The Andy Williams Show*. But, even with all that exposure, the LP only broke the top 50 on the *Billboard* Top 200 chart. Truthfully, there probably wasn't really anything song-wise that was strong enough to be a hit, including the songs I had written. We didn't tour with the record, instead playing just two gigs—the first one at the Santa Monica Civic Auditorium and the second one at New York's Fillmore East.

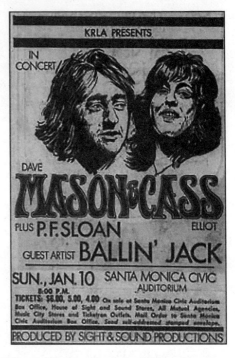

We remained close friends until her untimely death in 1974, a heart attack at the age of 32. That one album was our only collaboration. The last time I saw Cass, we were all in London together, shortly before she died. I was sad when I learned of her passing. Her home had been such a sanctuary for me, and I truly loved her. People ask me about our record together all the time. I always wonder what would've happened to Cass's career had she lived longer. It's easy for me to imagine her holding court on a politically incorrect talk show of her own. She had a wicked sense of humor. There was nobody like Cass.

One of the people who was hanging around a lot during this time was a guy named Billy Doyle, whom I mentioned earlier. He was part of the entourage and became a sort of de facto manager for me before the album with Cass was recorded. He was from Toronto, which is where I went to work with him after Cass and I finished the album. We shared a coach house, along with a man named Charles Tacot.

Honestly, those guys scared the hell out of me, and I couldn't believe what I had gotten myself into. Charles, for one, never went anywhere without a pistol. Like so many others around me, these two guys were heavily, *deeply* involved in drugs—cocaine, heroin, speed, you name it. Either through my own ignorance or stupidity, I managed to fall in with these people who came from the drug world. I remember, not long before the Manson murders, Doyle came back to Cass's house from Sharon Tate's house, and someone had beat the living shit out of him. He was wild and wanted to go back and murder everybody at that house. Charles Tacot chained him to a tree in Cass's garden for a day or two until he calmed down. It was like that. Always dark and crazy, and I was living in a near-constant state of vigilance in Canada. Later, too.

It started to become an unworkable situation. I began extricating myself. I retained an attorney named Brian Rohan to get myself separated from them as well as get all my songwriting and publishing royalties from the album with Cass.

For some reason, Rohan let the suit go into default. I retained yet another attorney, this time a prominent New York litigator. Either through my own negligence or where I was in the pecking order on his list, he let me go into what was now a double default.

What did that mean? The case was moved back to California, in Marin County Court. I didn't know what double default meant, and I showed up to find I'd lost the right to defend myself.

The gavel came down and adjudicated on Doyle's side. All my royalties are still, to this day, somewhere in Canada. It was an expensive education, and worse, I'd gotten involved with these characters and didn't know how to get out. Finally, I said, "Fuck it," walked away from all of it, and filed for bankruptcy. It was an unfortunate ending to an album that was a beautiful experience to make.

After the release of the album with Cass Elliot, Lorraine, our baby boy True, and I went back to London in the spring of 1971. Though we had a son together, Lorraine and I were on-again, off-again; frankly, I'd married her primarily out of obligation, which doesn't make for solid footing at home. I loved True, of course, but I was not cut out for a traditional family. For better or worse, my music took precedence, and of that, too, I wasn't quite sure what my next move was going to be. I had probably squandered

some momentum coming off *Alone Together* by doing the Cass Elliot
project, and I was drifting a bit.

One night not long after we'd settled in London, at the behest of
Lorraine, we paid a call to Chris Wood. I had not been in touch with the
other guys from Traffic, and I never expected in a million years that they
might be around. Steve lived out in Cheltenham, and Jim was in Evesham.

Coincidentally, they were both at Chris's. There, in that small flat, the
four original members of Traffic were unexpectedly together once again.
The mood was slightly tense at first, as we all still had some baggage, but
some hash joints instantly made things more comfortable. One thing led
to another, and then some acoustic instruments were pulled out, and we
started loosely jamming. We began telling some old stories, and all of
a sudden, the unlikely seemed at least semi-possible. A Traffic reunion?
Again! *Alone Together* had established me as a solo artist, and though I had
made a misstep with the duet album, there was still plenty of attention.
Perhaps I was still unsure about the idea of being a solo artist. I still fancied
myself as just another member in a band, and being in Traffic had allowed
me to validate that feeling. What can I say except I loved it in spite of it all.

I soon found myself in rehearsals for a short tour of colleges that
Traffic was doing. The band had expanded since I was last in it; it was now
a seven piece. In addition to us four originals, it also featured Jim Gordon
on drums, Rick Grech on bass, and Rebop Kwaku Baah on percussion. It
was a great lineup—hell, I even got to play some of my solo work in the
set. It felt good to be playing with them again; I was content, so I just kept
quiet as things progressed.

The short run of shows was set to begin at Central Polytechnic in
London the first week of May with a gig that also featured Soft Machine.
Then we played Liverpool Stadium. It was the next show, June 6 at
Fairfield Halls, Croydon, that was recorded for a live album. As I learned
later, the band's record label at that point, United Artists/Island, wanted a
live record that featured some of the old music that I'd played on. It didn't
hurt the cause that I'd just had a hit album with *Alone Together.*

The most memorable show we did was on the summer solstice. It
was called Glastonbury Fair, and it had been planned out by two people:
Andrew Kerr and Arabella Churchill. Arabella was Winston Churchill's
granddaughter. Because the organizers felt that music festivals were
becoming too commercialized, they decided there would be no entrance
fee at the site. Located in the British countryside about ten miles south of

a town called Downhead, the presentation took on a medieval tradition of music, poetry, dance, theater, and more. The festival had begun the previous year and had been successful enough for a second year. A large pyramid-shaped stage was erected, the first of its kind and now an iconic element of the festival that, by the way, is still going strong. In addition to Traffic, the 1971 version of Glastonbury also featured David Bowie, Hawkwind, Joan Baez, and Fairport Convention, among other artists.

On that tour, I brought out two of the most magnificent and expensive guitars I've ever owned in my life, a matching set of acoustic Martin D-45s—one a six-string, and one a twelve-string—beautifully inlaid with a mother of pearl binding and a Tree of Life on each fret board. The guitars were sitting on stands up against the amplifiers by the side of the pyramid stage.

Our set was going well, the music was flowing, and the crowd loved us. Then things unexpectedly intensified during "Dear Mr. Fantasy." After that, we closed the show with a raucous version of "Gimme Some Lovin." During that last song, the audience got out of hand. People started climbing up on stage; it was total chaos. Then, because of all those people on stage, the wall of amplifiers and the PA system began to sway back and forth before crashing in a massive heap. Thankfully, nobody was hurt, but those two precious guitars of mine were smashed to bits. We kept playing, but sadly, those guitars became something of a metaphor for any future plans I had with Traffic. I think we did one more show, and that was it. Within just a couple of months, the live recording from Croydon was released. It was called *Welcome to the Canteen*. I would get up on stage only a couple of times over the next few years to join Steve, Jim, and Chris for a song or two. It was over. But in my heart, I guess it's never been over.

Lorraine, our son True, and I went back to the US. I needed a course correction. I hired a manager in the San Francisco Bay Area, where we moved to—a man named Don Sherman. I started getting a band together. Soon, we would be recording another album.

Headkeeper

He seeks and he hides, he lives and he dies
He saw it before we were dreaming
He'll hustle you down, a tin can or a crown
But he'll never play with your feelings

Headkeeper's the name, he's been here since you came
And he's keeping ahead of the meaning
Headkeeper's the name, he's been here since you came
And he's keeping ahead of the meaning

He's weak and he's brave, he'll make you a slave
Or free you to fly in the heavens
With thoughts that are pure, he'll reflect all you saw
And all that is just an illusion

Don't you know the feeling, don't you know the truth
Don't you know you're dreaming, don't you know it's you
Don't you know it's you, don't you know it's you

Headkeeper's the name, he's been here since you came
And he's keeping ahead of the meaning
Headkeeper's the name, he's been here since you came
And he's keeping ahead of the meaning

He seeks and he hides, he lives and he dies
He saw it before we were dreaming
He'll hustle you down, a tin can or a crown
But he'll never play with your feelings

Don't you know the feeling, don't you know the truth
Don't you know you're dreaming, don't you know it's you
Don't you know it's you, don't you know it's you

CHAPTER NINE

Headkeeper

The new recording sessions, again at Sunset Sound, were starting to come together well. The title song, "Headkeeper," had turned out better than I'd hoped. A little different, given the fact that I didn't have the same players like Leon Russell and the others, though still very much in the acoustic guitar–electric guitar vein, like *Alone Together*. I had cut an earlier version of "Headkeeper" prior to these sessions, with Stevie Wonder playing drums. Though he laid down a great drum track, I wasn't happy with the arrangement, hence the re-do. (An agent I knew at CAA had connected us after I expressed an interest in working with Stevie.) Conceptually, I was planning on a double LP—a studio album of original material and a live show recorded at The Troubadour.

At this point, because of the success of *Alone Together,* I felt it was appropriate to renegotiate my recording agreement. Like I said earlier, Blue Thumb Records was a boutique label, in the vein of Blackwell's Island. Traffic had been a big part of the early days of Island's success, so certain promises were made by Chris that there would be a sharing of profits if Island Records was ever sold. Like most promises in this emerging world of rock and roll, the proverbial check was in the mail. When Island sold its publishing arm to A&M Records, of which "Feelin' Alright?" and all my other Traffic material was a part, nothing ever materialized. I was twenty-four years old and was tired of being taken advantage of. I was pissed. I went to Sunset Sound, walked right in, took all my master tapes for *Headkeeper,* and drove them to a vault in Sausalito. Yeah, I know. Bad move. I naively thought this would be leverage.

My renegotiation attempt took place in Blue Thumb's Rodeo Drive offices. Going to Blue Thumb in those days was not unlike scenes in *Scarface* where there were colossal piles of cocaine on desks, just there for the taking. My negotiation with Bob Krasnow, who was the president, went nowhere. We were at a standstill, neither side was giving in, and I still had the tapes. Meanwhile, unbeknownst to me, the label had taken unmixed copies of the recordings, which I'd forgotten about, and started compiling an album, eventually putting out an LP called *Dave Mason Is Alive* without my permission. One side of the album was made up of original studio recordings, and the other side showcased *unmixed* recordings from the Troubadour show. I was beside myself. Business is one thing, but fucking with my work, my music, my vision? At that point I dropped any renegotiation conversations and, in no uncertain terms, told Krasnow I wanted off the label and to work out some kind of override for a new label deal.

Blue Thumb was being distributed by Gulf and Western, based out of New York. I set up a meeting with the president of Gulf and Western, Tony Martell, in his top-floor office at the company's Manhattan office building. High stakes. I explained the situation and, in no ambiguous terms, demanded to be released from the label.

"If someone doesn't let me off this label," I said, "then I'll take my cause to the press regarding what's happening with the *Headkeeper* album."

Their lead attorney, also in attendance at the meeting, leapt out of his chair and yelled, "Are you threatening us?"

I guess he thought this was just a little artist that could be intimidated. I looked him square in the eye and said, "This is not a threat. It's a *promise.*"

And a promise it was. I did go to the press and told people not to buy my own record.

The only thing I would miss about Blue Thumb was my relationship with Tommy LiPuma, who had coproduced *Alone Together* with me. Tommy was one of the good guys. As for those original masters of *Headkeeper* tapes? Where are they? What happened to them? For the life of me, I do not know. But I sure wish I did.

In early 1972, I hit the road with most of my *Headkeeper* band: Mark Jordan on keyboards, Rick Jaeger on drums, Lonnie Turner on bass, Rocky Dzidzornu on congas, and a group of sisters from the Bay Area

named Anita, June, and Bonnie Pointer, also known as The Pointer Sisters.
I knew they would be big on their own someday, so I loved having them
out with us as background singers to help give our set a more soulful
edge. The first show The Pointer Sisters sang with me was at Winterland
in San Francisco. Opening for me that night, among others, were Loggins
& Messina and Taj Mahal. Bill Graham always had the knack of giving
people their money's worth.

**With my band (standing, L-R): Rocky Dzidzornu,
Mark Jordan, Rick Jaeger, and Lonnie Turner**

Let It Go, Let It Flow

When I'm alone I sometimes get to thinking
How it's gonna be when we're gone
Are we moving closer together
Or is it gonna take for ever and ever?

Let it go (let it go), let it flow like a river
Let it go (let it go), let it flow through you
Let it go (let it go), let it flow like a river
Let it go (let it go), let it flow through you

Searchin' everywhere just tryin' to find the reason
For misunderstanding and doubt
Don't wanna preach it, push it or teach it
Just take a good look all around

Let it go (let it go), let it flow like a river
Let it go (let it go), let it flow through you
Let it go (let it go), let it flow like a river
Let it go (let it go), let it flow through you

Walls are gonna fall and an angel's gonna call on you
To help you on your way
Time spent together, like now is forever
So don't ever let this love slip away

Let it go (let it go), let it flow like a river
Let it go (let it go), let it flow through you
Let it go (let it go), let it flow like a river
Let it go (let it go), let it flow through you

CHAPTER TEN

Let It Go, Let It Flow

In the summer of 1973, I started working on what felt like a comeback record. It was the first legitimate solo album I'd done since *Alone Together* since I don't really count *Headkeeper*. With the insanity and legal hot water from my breakup with Blue Thumb Records behind me, I was now on Columbia Records with someone that I still have a lot of respect for, Clive Davis. He's the reason I signed with them.

It's Like You Never Left was the title of my first album at Columbia. A big part of the story of this project is the incredible guest cast. Graham Nash sang harmony, and Stevie Wonder contributed beautiful harmonica on the song "The Lonely One." George Harrison (listed as Son of Harry on the record) played guitar on "If You've Got Love." Jim Keltner played drums on at least four of the tracks, and Rick Jaeger—who remained with me for the next eighteen years—played drums on the rest. Carl Radle played bass on a couple of the tracks, and I even had some interesting Moog programming by a man named Malcolm Cecil. He, along with Bob Margulies, coproduced the album.

My recording sessions with Malcolm and Bob would back up into the project they were working on in addition to mine, which was Stevie Wonder's *Songs in the Key of Life*. I would often come early to watch Stevie lay down drums, vocals, and piano. He was doing it all! Interestingly enough, though blind, Stevie would always walk around the mic stands in the room. He never bumped into them. His sensitivity was razor sharp; what a truly amazing man he is.

The first song on my album, "Baby . . . Please," is still requested often at live performances. I've tended to shy away from doing it, as the song is not about an unrequited love affair, as most people think. It's an ode to cocaine.

Staring out of windows like a helpless child
Pouring down the whiskey like it's goin' out of style
Trying to tell myself that everything is fine
In a big rubber room with a silver spoon still on my mind

Cocaine was becoming an even bigger part of my life then—and now my art. I've wondered if my severe introvert status as a youth was somehow a reason that I took to cocaine in the first place, in that it brought me out of my shell. That song was a tribute to its effect on me.

By 1974, my solo career was getting stronger, not because of hit records but because of engaging albums and word of mouth about the strength of my live performances. I went to Japan for a spell, but it was America where my bonds were strongest. I played hundreds of shows—in colleges, arenas, stadiums, amphitheaters, theaters, you name it.

Dave Mason, my second solo record for Columbia, came out that same year. The cover photo (as well as the image on the back, which was of the whole band) was shot on the veranda of the home I was renting in Bel Air. It was a really beautiful place with a view of ornate and manicured gardens, one of them belonging to the Kirkeby Mansion, which you might know from the opening of the TV series *The Beverly Hillbillies.* That said, it's not the cover I originally wanted. My original concept

was to go to the wonderfully eccentric artist Salvador Dali, who would, I hoped, do the artwork. Lorraine and I were in Manhattan, and somehow she got friendly with a member of his entourage, who got me a meeting with Dali. I'm not easily impressed by who someone is or what they do, but Dali was a true original, entirely in a league of his own. He always stayed at the St. Regis Hotel while he was in Manhattan, which is where we met, in his suite. I was like a nervous kid as I sang him a couple of my songs from the album. We spent an hour or so with him and his wife Gala. I was so enraptured by his larger-than-life presence that, by the time I left, the idea of him doing the artwork was secondary to the experience of meeting him. Sadly, he passed on the project. I guess I just didn't impress him. Still, to this day, I don't miss an opportunity while in St. Petersburg, Florida, to go to the Dali Museum. In 2008, I was inducted into The Order of Salvador, which, in true Dali spirit, is not to be taken too seriously.

The A&R department at Columbia Records was high on the song "Every Woman," which had been on the previous Columbia album *It's Like You Never Left.* It was an acoustic version that had Graham Nash singing the harmonies with me. They felt if I recut it with a full band, it could be a hit record. I was OK with that, and since I had such a great band in place from all the touring, I figured the entire album would come together easily. I still had Rick Jaeger. And now, in addition, I had

Jim Krueger, who was an outstanding guitar player as well as a splendid harmony singer. I also had Mike Finnigan, a 6'2" boy from Kansas. This guy could sing and play his ass off. His version of "Going Down Slow," which we did live, speaks for itself. A young boy of only nineteen, Bob Glaub, was our bass player.

The mores for the times were changing—in my life, in rock and roll, and in the world itself. I had a song on the album called "Show Me Some Affection." One of the lines was "I may be just an easy touch and taken for a whore."

"'Whore!' You can't use that word," said the execs at Columbia Records.

Oh no, not another artistic battle, I thought to myself.

Finally, I acquiesced. It wasn't worth the hassle since the album was almost finished. In order for it to rhyme in the song, I changed it to, "I may be just an easy touch and taken for much more." Boring. But those were the times. (I still said "whore" when we played it live, though.)

The album did pretty well. It hit number twenty-five on the *Billboard* pop chart, but there was still no breakthrough single. Despite that fact, I was playing to sellout crowds wherever we went. To the fans, hit records didn't seem to matter. But I was starting to get the feeling that the record label staff was getting impatient.

The band and I were on the road all the time. My marriage to Lorraine, though still legal, was over. She'd taken True and moved to Holland. I was all about the road, and I loved playing live. And the more we played, the more seasoned and comfortable I became onstage. The band made it so easy; they were that good.

Graham Nash is an acclaimed musician, singer, and songwriter and a member of the Hollies and Crosby, Stills & Nash. He and Dave are friends.

Graham Nash:
Dave came to visit me at my house in San Francisco in 1970. I had a studio in the basement and was just starting my album Songs for Beginners. *I'd already written "Military Madness" and played Dave the song. I asked him to put some guitar on the track. As a fine lead guitar player, I knew he'd know what to do. My best friend Joel Bernstein (archivist for Joni, Dylan, Neil, and Prince) was fooling*

around in the studio on piano, which he played on the record. Dave came and sat down with him on the same piano stool and played his guitar to great effect.

Later, Dave played me a demo of a new song he'd written, "Every Woman," and I immediately knew that I could add my harmony voice to his beautiful song. I've always enjoyed singing with him. Dave's been a friend for a long, long time. I sang on stage with him in NYC in a show play remembering Ahmet Ertegun, who had just passed away after falling in the bathroom of the Beacon Theater while watching The Rolling Stones.

Show Me Some Affection

To some I am a blessing, to others I'm a curse
I'm a writer, not a fighter, I'm a person not a purse
I may be just an easy touch, taken for a whore
But I just came to leave a little lovin' at your door

Ohhh, show me some affection
Ohhh, give me some direction
Ohhh, you know you're my connection

Just a jet age gypsy looking for a gypsy queen
I sometimes think I'm on the brink of knowing what I mean
Cities come and cities go but still I cannot find
A place to call my home when there's a woman on my mind

Ohhh, show me some affection
Ohhh, give me some direction
Ohhh, you know you're my connection

If hanging out with you was spent in hanging in
I'd still be out of time with time just waiting to begin
I have no preconceived ideas of how things have to be
I'll just take life as it comes and hope that it takes me

Ohhh, show me some affection
Ohhh, give me some direction
Ohhh, you know you're my connection

CHAPTER ELEVEN
Show Me Some Affection

The *Split Coconut* album (1975) was named after a Jamaican restaurant located in a funky basement in London. It was more of a bar than a restaurant, really, and my bandmates from Traffic and I used to go there, especially for the jerk chicken, strong drinks, and maybe a little ganja thrown in.

Graham Nash was back for that album to provide those beautiful harmonies of his. And speaking of harmonies, I also had David Crosby, a voice I've always loved. The members of Manhattan Transfer, who at the time were doing this wartime bebop that was so cool, came in to add

their flavor to the songs. I did a cover on this album, "Crying, Waiting, Hoping," originally done by Buddy Holly, who I regret I never got to see perform live.

I think the most special song on the album was "Give Me a Reason." It was a song I wrote for True, who at that time was four, maybe five years old. I wasn't around to help raise him; I was touring all the time. The road made these things tough. But I thought about True a whole lot, and as a songwriter, I figured if I couldn't see him that much, I could at least write him a song, and that would

last forever. Missing my son inspired this song, and though it's written
for True, it's a song for anyone who has a child at that inquisitive age of
wonder.

For the *Split Coconut* tour, I duplicated the album cover as the
backdrop for our stage show. I also had some fake palm trees sitting
around. I painted all the equipment lights blue. The only thing missing on
stage was a bar serving piña coladas! This helped create a mood; I mean,
tours were already a party, but this island vibe just amped it up.

As much fun as I was having on the road at that time, there is another
side of the coin: things were not well internally. I'd let my finances get into
a mess, my indulgences were deep, and my ways of excess were catching
up with me. *Baby… please, you got me scraping on my knees,* indeed.

I needed help, career-wise and in many other ways too.

Like many things in life, an answer appeared as if out of left field. His
name was Jason Cooper, and he was a large, affable man who had hair
down to his ass and was always dressed in Hawaiian shirts and shorts. I
met him through mutual friends at a time when he was watching over
two young heirs, Bobby Sullivan, heir to Wells Fargo, and Danny Briggs,
heir to Stauffer Chemicals, who only talked to trees and Bobby Sullivan.
Both of them were wannabe movie makers who had backed the film *Myra
Breckinridge*. They were renting a house in Mandeville Canyon that had
once belonged to Esther Williams and, of course, had a magnificent pool.
I visited a few times and once had dinner there with Mae West, who was
starring in *Myra Breckinridge*. Though a sex symbol in her own time, I got
the distinct impression she was a man in drag.

While Jason was employed there, we became friendly. Mind you, he
had no music management experience, but through our friendship I felt
more confident in having someone like him represent me. Which is a bold
choice, to be sure, because at that point I had garnered enough success
that there were several options of picking somebody within the industry.
Trust was a big issue with me in those days after my experience with
Chris Blackwell at Island Records and Bob Krasnow of Blue Thumb—
experiences that to this day continue to challenge my trust in relationships
within the business. But I trusted Jason, and with a good deal of thought
about it and a big leap of faith, I hired him as my manager. For better or
worse, I rely on gut instinct for many decisions. This maverick method of
self-management hasn't always worked out for me, but in this case it did.
Jason was the most successful manager of my career to date and went on

to do good things for others, like Ron Wood, whom he managed for a time after me.

Out of the blue in July 1975, Jason told me that he'd been contacted by Bob Dylan's people. Bob wanted me to join him in a New York City studio where he was in the initial stages of working out the tracks that would become his next album, *Desire*. This was right around the time he was hatching the concept for the revolutionary gypsy caravan tour called *The Rolling Thunder Revue* that would happen later in the year. I didn't know what to expect once we got there, but this was Bob Dylan. I was a huge fan, and one of my fondest memories growing up—and which you might recall—was seeing him go electric with The Band back in London in the mid-1960s. That night blew a lot of minds and pissed off a lot of diehard folk fans. But I loved it.

When I got to the studio, it was a situation reminiscent of Harrison's All Things Must Pass sessions whereby there were a number of players on the scene and no formal structure to the sessions. It was all very loose. Bob had other session players there, along with a woman name Scarlet Rivera, the violin player who would ultimately become a member of Rolling Thunder. We laid down a couple of songs, including "Joey," which was about the gangster Joey Gallo, and "Rita Mae," which had been written about the writer Rita Mae Brown.

In that unscripted session as we were working, Bob intuitively leaned over and joked to me, "You're not used to working like this, are you?" And he was right.

As it happened, Cathy Nicholas was in the room, and after I'd done my parts on the songs, she looked a lot more interesting to me than hanging around in what became a musically confusing scene. I left with her. This began a longtime romance, which is in some ways a bigger standout memory of that day.

The next time I saw Bob, some years later at a gas station in Malibu—filling up his car near mine—he told me that he thought my song "Every Woman" was one of the most beautiful love songs ever written. This is a compliment I've never taken lightly, given that I consider Bob Dylan the Picasso of songwriters and one of the greatest lyricists of all time.

In the fall of that year—1975—Peter Frampton and I embarked on a short arena tour, marketed as a show featuring two prominent British guitarists. Peter opened the performances, and I closed. He and I played an enormous show earlier that summer in Oakland, "A Day on the Green,"

Cathy Nicholas, me, and my mother enjoying a night out.

along with Robin Trower and Fleetwood Mac. This was an era when stadium shows were starting to become popular, and I would frequently get booked on those bills. I may not have had the radio hits, but I definitely had a live audience and avid followers who seemed to appreciate what I did.

I also headlined Madison Square Garden in New York with Peter. I had not been there since that night in 1969 when we opened for Blind Faith. Now I was there as part of a headliner due, in no small part, to the sheer amount of work I'd done since that time: five albums and thousands of concerts. Frampton was coming into his own, and he was a dynamic opener who put on a fantastic live show. He had smartly been recording his concerts and was soon to release a little something called *Frampton Comes Alive.*

We were promoting the *Split Coconut* album and garnering audience support as well as good press. Even *The New York Times* gave us a nice review. It was starting to feel like I was on the cusp of something big, something that could rescue me from financial difficulties and establish me on solid footing as a commercial artist. I didn't know then, like I do today, the fleeting nature of fame.

From time to time, some special "guest" opportunities still came up. One night in 1975, when I was on tour in New Orleans, Wings guitarist Denny Laine came to see me perform at The Warehouse and told me afterward, "Come over to the studio tomorrow. I know Paul wants to see you."

Paul McCartney, of course. Who else is referred to as simply *Paul?* While I hadn't seen Paul for a while, we had history, much of which you know. It was good to catch up with him, but it was a much different situation than the first time when he came over and I met him at Carol Russell's house. Or when he sent me that telegram after hearing my song "Hole in My Shoe." Now we were about to be just two musicians working together.

There was a song he was working on in the studio called "Listen to What the Man Said." Paul played me the riff, handed me an electric guitar, and I played it with him. I added a little harmony part, which at first made him wince, but I said, "Wait, just listen to it again." He did, he liked it, and so he kept it.

And that became Paul and Wings' next number-one record. It was a moment, once again, of being in the right place at the right time and catching music firsthand that's now—well, there's only one word for it— *iconic.*

In the studio with Denny Laine and Paul McCartney.

For me, Paul remains one of the greatest songwriters and musicians of our generation. He's a true gentleman and was always generous with his time. I would often be welcomed backstage when our schedules coincided, and I well remember a party he threw on the Queen Mary in Long Beach Harbor—a super fun night of great music and food, where I spent much of the night unsuccessfully trying to get next to Cher's sister.

Jason Cooper was Dave's tour manager in the 1970s.

Jason Cooper:
A fellow named Danny Briggs had inherited a lot of money by the age of nineteen. He and his friend Bobby Sullivan were very young, and both wanted to get into film. Danny's mom had me down there, checking out what was going on and keeping an eye on him, and that's where I first met Dave Mason. He had just

released the album It's Like You Never Left, and I loved it. He was already kind of a legend. I mean, when you cofound a band like Traffic, that's always going to be a big deal in terms of history. But he had built lots of things on top of that. The Alone Together album was obviously a masterpiece, and though I know he had some weird legal situations in terms of releasing more music, by the time It's Like You Never Left came out, he was back on track, at least musically.

But there was a lot of chaos in his life in terms of management. It was actually a mess, and he really needed help. That blew my mind. How could a guy with this kind of talent be so poorly managed? Knowing what I know today, I get it. I get how the business works against an artist like Dave. But back then, I didn't know anything about the music business. Since he was in such a state, I was interested in doing whatever I could do to get him back on track. Did I ever think I would become Dave Mason's manager for the rest of the decade? No way. But sometimes you never know what's around the corner.

Dave and I got along well, and I guess he trusted me. He said one day, "Do you want to manage me?" Why the hell not? I mean, how much worse can it get? It was just the right time for him to make a move. I took the plunge and figured it out as I went along. I got to know the people at Columbia Records, and they were fine with everything. They welcomed me into my new role for the most part. We hit the road for a while, and then Dave got some new songs ready to make another album, which we did. That album was called simply Dave Mason, and it featured songs that were, for me, some of Dave's best songs ever.

In July 1975, I was contacted by Bob Dylan's management, and they wanted Dave to come to New York City to play a session with Bob. There were a lot of other musicians there, and Dave spent an afternoon playing with him, but nothing was ever used for the upcoming Dylan album, Desire. I think the best thing that happened at that session was that Dave met an amazing woman who would become his longtime girlfriend, Cathy. She was just beautiful, really lovely, and almost immediately she became part of our traveling circus.

Most of my fondest memories of Dave were from being on the road. There were so many times where I would just pinch myself. In September 1975, when Dave and the band played in London at the Hammersmith Odeon, Paul and Linda McCartney came to watch the show. They were standing next to me on the side of the stage during the concert, and Paul kept turning to say how great he thought the band was.

After the show, Dave set up an afterparty at a little Jamaican bar called Split Coconut. Most of us sampled some brownies at that party. They were hash brownies. Even me, who rarely drank and never touched drugs. At least when I knew what they were. We had a great time at the bar, but when it came time to leave, Dave insisted on driving us back to the hotel in a Rolls Royce we had rented. There was no way in hell I was letting him drive me, but he had to drive because no way was I driving on what for me was the wrong side of the road. That Rolls Royce spoke volumes about Dave's expensive tastes and style. He liked to enjoy himself and was never shy about spending money on things that he liked.

And, of course, it was the name of the club, Split Coconut, that inspired the title and album artwork theme of Dave's next release. Split Coconut came out in the fall 1975, and it was fairly well received both commercially and critically. It was great watching the recording sessions because Dave had his friends Graham Nash and David Crosby provide backing vocals, and Graham even played some guitar.

Much of our travel in the mid- to late 1970s was done on a private plane that Dave chartered from the country artist Charlie Rich. For the most part, it was great. We never had to rush to the airport, we never missed a flight, and the rules on board were, let's just say, "relaxed." That said, the single scariest moment of my life took place on board a plane in the fall of 1975. We had just finished playing a sold-out Madison Square Garden in New York City and were en route to the next gig, playing with The Beach Boys in Cincinnati. We had to use a different plane this time, a Convair 580, a large twin-engine piston plane. Halfway through the flight, the cabin started to fill up with smoke. Rock 'n' roll obviously has a bad history with planes, whether we're talking about Buddy Holly or Otis Redding or Lynyrd Skynyrd, among others. I thought our number was up.

It turned out there was an oil leak in the heating system on the plane. We had to make an emergency landing somewhere in West Virginia. Somehow, the pilot found a remote airstrip and managed to get the plane down safely, although all the tires were torn off by the time the craft came to a stop. It was truly harrowing. Some of the people on board were saying their prayers as the plane shook and rocked throughout the entire descent. But we managed to get out of there alive, charter another plane, and make it to the gig only an hour behind schedule.

Another memorable show on the road with Dave took place in Missouri, along with The Band, America, and several other acts on July 3, 1976, playing an outdoor festival at Chuck Berry's farm in Wentzville. Normally when an artist plays, you get paid half upfront, and then half either during or after the show is over. That was standard back in those days. We took two helicopters and landed at Berry's place. It was a zoo. The show looked oversold. There was no ticket booth, so someone hastily converted a port-a-potty into one. It was a hot summer day, the crowd was anxiously waiting for the music, and we were anxiously waiting to get paid. But that didn't happen. They told us we would get paid after the gig. Elliot Roberts (who was managing America at that time) told them we wouldn't go on until we received half upfront, but Berry's people balked. "Fuck it," Elliot said. "We're leaving. Come on everybody, let's get back in the helicopters." So that's what we did. Dave was with me and Elliot in the first helicopter, and there was one behind us. Just after we took off, we saw Chuck Berry's management "team" come running out from where we had just taken off. They had pistols and began shooting at us! As we flew away, we could hear the gunshots, and that's probably the second-scariest travel experience with Dave.

There were a lot of drugs going around back then. Even though that wasn't part of my personal world, as Dave's manager, I had to get involved sometimes when it came to the amounts of cocaine that were being consumed by Dave, the band, and other assorted hangers-on. But that was rock 'n' roll in the 1970s. I know coke still had its place in the '80s, '90s, and beyond, but the 1970s were a different story altogether. Cocaine was still considered simply a "recreational" drug, and nobody worried too much about being addicted to it.

Dave loved his custom-tailored suits, which cost a fortune. I remember one time after he bought that new house, he purchased a $22,000 Persian rug. I said to him, "Are you crazy? All that money for a rug?" He didn't care. He loved spending money, and he had very expensive taste. He also had great taste in everything, from furniture to clothing to drugs, to booze to furnishings to food to women. But it cost money. And sometimes you start spending more than you have coming in, and that's where the problems really start. He could be very stubborn and had the *answers to everything, and that became challenging after a while. But he's also an artist, and artists of course are sometimes known for being somewhat eccentric or demanding. As Dave's manager, I didn't let it get to me because I knew how talented he was. Whatever environment he had to create to be creatively successful, that's what interested me. After a while, the work became very hard. As I said, the drugs did not make it easy, but in the end, it was just time for me to move on. I'll always love Dave Mason. He allowed me an opportunity to get involved in the music business, and he's a remarkably talented artist who has very sweet and generous sides to him that not everybody gets to see. But I did.*

Baby . . . Please

I think I'll lose an hour or two with you beside the water
Don't lose time in bringing me that good thing that you ought to

Baby . . . please
You've got me scraping my knees
Baby . . . please
Please, please don't make me go back to the freeze

Every time that I try to connect, girl, well, it seems that your line is engaged
I'm a slave to the way that you move me, I'm a puppy dog wagging my tail

Baby . . . please
You've got me scraping my knees
Baby . . . please
Please, please don't make me go back to the freeze

Staring out of windows like a helpless child
Pouring down the whiskey like it's goin' out of style
Trying to tell myself that everything is fine
In a big rubber room with a silver spoon still on my mind

Well, I'm pacing the floor like a tiger, living nights that have passed into days
Looking over my shoulder to catch anything coming my way

Baby . . . please
You've got me scraping my knees
Baby . . . please
Please, please don't make me go back to the freeze

CHAPTER TWELVE

Baby . . . Please

We all know what happened when *Frampton Comes Alive* was unleashed in 1976. It was the bestselling album of 1976 and sold over eight million copies. And since we had been touring together during his recording of at least part of it, I was inspired to do a live album of my own. I'd been thinking about it for a while because I knew that I had one of the hottest live bands on the road, and I loved the energy of our shows in that era.

By 1975, we were as tight as a band could get. We were so locked in with one another that it allowed us to go off on all kinds of musical excursions: extending solos here, expanding sections there, very similar to what we'd been doing in Traffic's live shows. That essence of authenticity was what I craved to capture on record. It was, for me, exhilarating.

The Universal Amphitheater was a very cool venue to play on those warm LA nights. It was outdoors back then, and I was going to be performing there for two nights. Both shows were sold out, and a fairly new artist, Eddie Money, was opening. He was starting to get major attention with his record "Baby Hold On." I liked his music, and I liked Eddie personally.

Hanging out with Delaney Bramlett (L) and Eddie Money (R).

We also had some celebs in the audience, Tatum O'Neal being one of them. The setting was perfect, and because we were in one venue for

more than one night, it was also the perfect opportunity to record the shows.

I didn't want to put any overdubs on this record. I wanted it to be presented just as we played it. We had two great, memorable nights of music. The band was on fire, and so was the audience's reaction. When it came time to mix the record, I was presented with the chance to do it on a 150-foot boat that had been set up as a floating studio. For the same amount of time and money it would take to mix in a regular LA studio, I could do it on a yacht. Well, what to do? I went for the boat, of course. A working vacation for everybody.

I decided we would take the boat to Mexico, where we anchored off some small islands. Members of the band, wives, girlfriends, Cathy, and my mother all lived on that boat for two weeks. Swimming, diving, racing around on jet skis, eating fresh fish, living the life. And, of course, working every day on what would become the album *Certified Live*.

My mom joined us for the Certified Live festivities.

Without Ron Nevison, who was also on this working vacation and mixing the album, it would have never come together so easily. Ron kept me focused and was vital to this project as well as two other albums, *Let It Flow* and *Mariposa de Oro*.

Ron Nevison is a record producer and audio engineer. He was the engineer on *Certified Live*.

Ron Nevison:

I had been working in England for a number of years. I had the opportunity to work with some truly legendary artists, including The Who and Led Zeppelin. But then things started getting difficult over there. The Labor Government started forcing many artists out of the UK by taxing their out-of-the-country earnings. It became very cumbersome for many well-known artists, including The Rolling Stones, Rod Stewart, and Elton John, which meant that work for me was starting to dry up over there. I got a call from the Record Plant in Los Angeles to come back over to the States and take over as their chief engineer. I was excited. We worked out the details in late 1974, and by 1975, I was back home, working with even more terrific artists. One of those was Dave Mason.

In the later part of 1976, I got the call that I was going to be mixing a new live project that Dave had been working on. At first, I was surprised that Bruce Botnick was not called. After all, he had actually recorded the live shows himself. But whatever, sometimes that's just how it works out, perhaps from scheduling reasons or something else. I didn't care; either way, I was anxious to work on the project. What made it even more interesting was that Dave wanted to rent a minesweeper yacht for about two weeks to mix the record. I loved the idea, not just because it represented a chance to have some fun while working but also I had a lot of experience working remotely like that. I had worked in houses, other strange buildings, and all kinds of interesting, nontraditional spaces.

I met with Dave, and soon after, it was "all aboard" toward Todos Santos, a little town on the Pacific coast of Mexico's Baja California peninsula. Just a beautiful area, backed by the Sierra de Laguna Mountain Ridge. Once we got there, it was clear that everybody was going to have a good time. But there was work to do. The ship was equipped with a quad eight mixing console and a two-track tape machine. We could create a little reverb here and there if we wanted, but not much else. At first, I got freaked out trying to mix on a boat.

There were plenty of distractions, including swimming and going into town on skiff boats certain days. Dave's girlfriend, the lovely Cathy, was along, and she was delightful, as was Dave's mother. I thought it was so unique that she was there, and she and Dave clearly were very close. She fit right in; clearly, she had adapted to the rock 'n' roll lifestyle. I really liked her.

Maybe it was the red wine or some other substances, but the bottom line was we really didn't have to fix anything on those recordings. That's why we called it Certified Live. What you heard was what you got. It was an authentic live record, and even though the band wasn't needed, they all appreciated the break from the road.

Once we got home, I kind of freaked out again when it came to mastering the record because the highs and lows were all over the place. I started getting concerned that it had sounded better while we were on the boat. But once we settled in, it came back to me that this really was an authentic live record that had been recorded beautifully with wonderful players. It really hadn't needed much of anything. I think we were all very proud of that record when it came out. It seemed to capture the magic that wonderful band put forth onstage every night.

I guess because we had such a great experience, it was natural for me to work on Dave's next album, Let it Flow. I remember when Dave brought in the song "We Just Disagree." This guitar player, the wonderful Jim Krueger, had written it, and Dave really loved the song.

When it came to material, Dave didn't have any ego. He didn't care where the song came from as long as it was a good song. "So High (Rock Me Baby and Roll Me Away)" had been cowritten by Mentor Williams, who also penned "Drift Away" for Dobie Gray. I brought that one to Dave. Great song. Dave himself had written some great songs for the album, including the title track and "Mystic Traveler."

That album, of course, represented Dave's first truly big solo commercial hit record, thanks to "We Just Disagree." But it was just a beautiful package overall. Great cover concept. The label printed a bunch of clear blue vinyl, which really fit the mood of the album—free, easy, and on the open water. Just a wonderful record. It really elevated Dave as well. The only problem when you have a hit record, at least in my opinion, it gets harder to write great songs because you don't have as much conflict in your life. You need bad times, I think, to write great songs.

Looking back, I really loved working with Dave Mason because he is a true artist. Yes, he may have been caught up in a lot of the rock star trappings that many people were into back then, but for him, it always came back to the music. He was always very focused in the studio and really cared about what he was doing and what the band was doing. He had a great ear for music and a great lust for life, and that working experience remains one of my favorite memories of the late 1970s.

Mystic Traveler

Hanging in a crystal tree, a love light shines for all to see
'Cause in our hearts we know the way it goes
Sharing all that we can give, and living all that we can live
With freedom as our only cornerstone

Mystic traveler, he's the unraveller
And he will always bring you safely home
Mystic traveler, he's the unraveller
And when he's in your heart, you're not alone
And when he's in your heart, you're not alone

Time is on our side I feel, the light of truth will soon reveal
A reason for our fears of letting go
All of our life's energy is flowing between you and me
We're together though we're quite alone

Mystic traveler, he's the unraveller
And he will always bring you safely home
Mystic traveler, he's the unraveller
And when he's in your heart, you're not alone
And when he's in your heart, you're not alone

No more sailing on a sea of broken-hearted memories
Understanding is the key
Loving you can only be a love for all eternity
Too much time has passed, thank the Lord, you're here at last

Hanging in a crystal tree, a love light shines for all to see
'Cause in our hearts we know the way it goes
Sharing all that we can give, and living all that we can live
With freedom as our only cornerstone

Mystic traveler, he's the unraveller
And he will always bring you safely home
Mystic traveler, he's the unraveller
And when he's in your heart, you're not alone
And when he's in your heart, you're not alone

CHAPTER THIRTEEN

Mystic Traveler

As I said, I'd signed with Columbia Records because I had a tremendous deal of respect for the legendary record man, Clive Davis. While I was there, in 1973, Columbia ousted him on allegations of misuse of funds and providing drugs to artists and DJs. In my mind, these were trumped-up charges against a man who was becoming too powerful in a major organization. It was absurd on its face since the entire industry was doing the same thing.

I'd come from an era where one man's decision in a company would make a difference between things happening and not happening. The corporate world was moving to an age of consensus, which I had—and have—to question.

Clive Davis went on to form Arista Records and become hugely successful with an innovative roster of artists, sell millions of records, and make a lasting mark in the music industry. I know from experience what happens when you lose a champion of your art, and I lost my biggest ally at Columbia. When Clive left, I wasn't feeling supported by the label—even after doing three albums, not to mention all the touring. Coupled with the fact that my priority was to always put on a first-rate live show, the cost of touring, plus—and I'll be the first to admit it—my own neglect, I was spending more than I was making. It all led to me filing my second bankruptcy.

If I filed bankruptcy, under the law I could get out of my contract with Columbia because all of your contracts are null and void. This was

well and fine with me since Clive was no longer there. This put me in a
position to be the first artist ever to break a contract by filing bankruptcy.

Of course, this move led me into a direct fight with Columbia
Records. As I was walking out of the hearing one day, the Columbia
attorney stopped me in the hallway, looked at me, and said, "We're going
to bury you." I took this to mean, among other things, my career was over
in the music industry.

Yet, I didn't blink, and eye to eye, I replied, "To make that kind of
threat, you must be running scared. Take your best shot." And they did.

Columbia took everything I had left, which wasn't much, really. The
only thing I really had was my Mercedes Benz, so I didn't even have a
car after they were done with me. In fact, the judge looked at me with a
smug stare during the proceedings and said, "Oh, we're going to take that
too." I was living at the Marina del Ray Towers at the time. I went home
after court, got into the car, and drove the Mercedes into the wall. I just
destroyed it. Okay, there is your *fucking car.*

At one of my lowest points, what I remember most is that I'd found
an ally in Ahmet Ertegun, president at Atlantic Records. I wanted to work
with Ahmet desperately, and he was very interested in signing me. Since
I was broke, he graciously lent me $50,000 out of his personal account.
(I eventually paid him back.) And while the attorneys at Atlantic's parent
company, Warner Bros., were working to sort through my bankruptcy
and broken contract situation with Columbia, Ahmet invited me to join
him on a trip to Europe for three weeks. He was working on signing The
Rolling Stones.

I took my girlfriend Cathy and her friend Mara, and we joined Ahmet
on the Warner jet. Off we went to Europe—London, Paris, Brussels,
Germany—attending Stones concerts while going to the best restaurants,
the coolest nightclubs, and staying in the finest hotels. It only made me
want to be with Ahmet and Atlantic Records even more. Not only was
Ahmet Ertegun a great record man, but he had a lot of style and class.

When we got back from the trip, much to my dismay, Ahmet
said that since there was no precedent for breaking a label contract
through bankruptcy, their legal department wouldn't allow me to join
Atlantic. Meanwhile, back at Columbia Records, Jason had arranged a
renegotiation. Ahmet encouraged me to take that deal. So I did. And it was
back to Columbia Records I went.

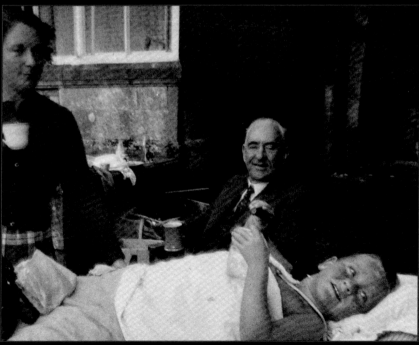

Even though I sometimes had to wear a tie and be a good school boy,
I grew up with a spirit of adventure like Huckleberry Finn. I loved being
outdoors, even during the time I was confined at the hospital.

**Obsessed with Hank Marvin and ready to become
a teenaged rock & roll guitar slinger!**

Traffic's early days: Chris Wood, Steve Winwood, Jim Capaldi, and me.

The late 1960s was a great era to be a young musician. Music and fashion went together like never before, and we felt like we were changing the world.

This photo was snapped at the Traffic cottage when photographer Linda Eastman (the future Mrs. Paul McCartney) came out for a visit.

I've had the opportunity to make music with some incredibly talented
friends, including Jimi Hendrix (above), and my brief stint with
Eric Clapton in an early version of Derek and the Dominoes (below).
This was the one and only concert I played as a Domino! The shot with
Jimi was taken in my apartment at around 7 AM. We were still jamming!

This contact sheet offers a glimpse into a fun photo session
with my friend, photographer Barry Feinstein.

Mama Cass Elliot was a good friend, and I so enjoyed making music with her. Here we are with Ned Doheny before our planned trio became a duo of just me and Cass.

One of my great band lineups in the 1970s (L-R, standing): Rocky Dzidzornu, Mark Jordan, Rick Jaeger, and Lonnie Turner.

Recording with Wings at Allen Toussaint's studio in New Orleans in 1975 (L-R): Linda McCartney, Joe English, Denny Laine, me, and Paul McCartney.

Life was moving fast in the 1970s. There were a lot of gigs, which meant I didn't get to spend as much time with my son True (upper right) as I wish I had. Being around him always brought me a lot of joy.

Another great band lineup from the 1970s
(L-R): Jay Wynding, Gerald Johnson, and Rick Jaeger.

The night Traffic was inducted into the Rock & Roll Hall of Fame.
(Above) Jamming with Billy Gibbons, Keith Richards, and others on
"Feelin' Alright?" (Below) Backstage with Jim Capaldi, Kid Rock,
Jackson Browne, Keith Richards, Steve Winwood, and Tom Petty.

One of the reasons I got into this business was to let loose on the electric guitar, and I still love it!

With my beautiful daughter, Danielle.

Still Road Dogs after all these years. I love getting out there with the band and feeling the energy of all you beautiful friends in the audience. There's nothing like the power of live music.

My legal troubles hadn't hurt my relationship with the public in the least, and I'd been appearing regularly on many TV shows, including hosting *The Midnight Special*. My albums always did well, but like I said, my connection with the audience was really through my live shows. I would get played a lot on FM radio, but there wasn't that breakout hit, that song that would become so identifiable that the whole country finds itself humming it.

That changed in 1977 when I did an album called *Let It Flow*, my first album after re-signing with Columbia and my biggest-selling album to date.

My longtime band member Jim Krueger was visiting me at my house in Mariposa and told me he'd written a song that he thought was just perfect for me. He sat down on the couch with his acoustic guitar and started playing me this song that, hit or no hit, was to me a really beautiful song. I mentioned earlier that there's an old adage in my business that says it's all about the song, the song, the song. And even though I had written my own songs that were hits for me or hits for other people, it would be this song, written by Jim Krueger, that would become my biggest hit single: "We Just Disagree." What struck me most about the song was that it felt like something I would or could have written myself. Jim said he wrote it with me specifically in mind, and he nailed it.

Onstage with bassist Gerald Johnson and Jim Krueger.

The crowds knew the words almost immediately, and it became an anthem of sorts. Plus, it helped fuel the lifestyle that I was pushing harder and harder. I had a hit record. And with that came all the spoils. I mean, having a hit just pushes it all into another dimension. I was diving deeper and deeper into the LA scene, where I lived in that era. What they say about the party scene in those days is true one hundredfold. And frankly, a lot of that time is blurry. Some of it was the drugs. Some of it was the fast-paced tour life, and hell, sometimes it was just life in general. It was a lot of fun, new and old faces weaving in and out—like a party at the home of Wendy Stark, the daughter of famed Hollywood producer Ray Stark, where every star you can imagine was in attendance.

One night, an attractive blonde came over and asked, "Don't you remember me?"

I had to rack my brain. By then there had been so many. I didn't remember her, and I was embarrassed. "Do I owe you an apology?" I joked, trying to cover the moment.

"Dave," she said to me, locking her eyes on mine, "It's me, Suze. You used to pull my pigtails when we were kids."

Oh, my God. Susan Randall! The little girl I grew up next door to. She had made a name for herself as a *Playboy* photographer and was considered one of the most provocative photographers of her era. And here she was. I exhaled. I couldn't believe how our paths had brought us both to this point. I couldn't believe how life, just when you thought your feet wouldn't hit the ground again, intervenes to remind you: it's just me here. David Thomas Mason from Worcester, England.

At the time, I had split with Cathy and was dating the actress Leigh Taylor Young, with whom I had some history. On and off over the years we would get together and always shared a close bond and friendship, even to this day. Leigh was very involved with a spiritual community called Movement for Spiritual Inner Awareness (MSIA). Its leader was a man named John Roger, who the members referred to as the mystic traveler. And though I was never officially a member of the organization, I was drawn into it by default through my relationship with Leigh.

The term *mystic traveler* stuck with me. It was so fascinating, and it led me to write a song of the same title. And to keep me well protected while touring, it's currently the name of my tour bus.

Leigh Taylor-Young is an American actress and longtime girlfriend of Dave's. They remain close friends.

Leigh Taylor-Young:
I was deep in my spiritual practice at that time. In my home in Beverly Hills, I had a tiny guesthouse on the property. On a tree next to the house, I had about 150 crystals hanging delicately, reflecting all of the prismatic beauty of the sun. Dave loved sitting there with his guitar. In the shadow of the tree, among all of the reflections of the crystals, he would softly play his acoustic guitar, and I would sit there and listen to him. I had been telling him all about John Roger, the "mystical traveler of consciousness," whom I had been following. John was an author and founder of the movement of spiritual inner awareness as well as several other New Age, spiritual, and self-help organizations.

One day, Dave called me outside under the tree. "Sit down," he said. "I've written a song about the mystical traveler. I want to play it for you under the crystal tree."

After he finished, I couldn't believe how in tune and how in touch he was. The music and spirit of the music was a direct reflection of John Roger. The song was called "Mystic Traveler." Soon, thousands got to hear what would become the organization's theme song.

The song "Let It Go, Let It Flow," from which the album is titled, is one I wrote that, in many ways, is quintessential to my theory as a songwriter. While it's hard to remember what event actually inspired this song, it reminds me it's not so much about a specific moment in time but rather a broad, sweeping inspiration of quiet moments of reflection. *I get to thinking how it's going to be when we're gone.* Everlasting themes, good solid lyrics, and melodic music are the things I aspire to as an artist—then and to this day.

The artwork for the album jacket was the first time that I wasn't really involved in the design process. The art department at Columbia Records came up with it. At first, I didn't really like it, but it grew on me. And that's when I got involved by asking if we couldn't do something similar to *Alone Together,* meaning a colored vinyl. I thought there would be resistance from the label, but they were very much for it. We settled on a transparent blue, which reflected the theme of the cover. Like *Alone Together,* a special, limited edition of blue vinyl was printed. *Let It Flow* went on to become a platinum album. My first and only, though now it's probably gone on to even sell a lot more.

After finishing the album, it was time to go back on the road to promote it. The commercial success of "We Just Disagree" and the success of the album helped propel me to even bigger stages in the summers of 1977–79. And since the venues were larger and offers were plentiful, including an upcoming run of

forty-eight concerts in fifty-two days, it was time to have my own plane.

Though I was successful, I wasn't in the bracket to afford a full-size jet. My manager Jason Cooper went looking for the best options, and we finished up using country singer Charlie Rich's plane.

Margie Peeples was the flight attendant when Dave used Charlie Rich's plane during the late 1970s and remains a close friend of the family.

Margie Peeples:
I was working for the singer Charlie Rich as a flight attendant. Back then, the term flight attendant *was a lot different than it is today. If you were touring with a musician, you basically took care of*

everything. You got the food for the plane, you kept that plane clean, you made sure everyone in the band had what they needed, and anything else that came up in between. It was definitely a full-time job, but I loved it.

In the winter of 1976, Dave Mason leased the plane from Charlie. It was a British airplane, a Vickers Viscount, and Dave loved it. He was really into planes. Hank Conrad was the captain, and Marty Manger was the copilot. Initially, the tour was throughout the East Coast, and it was bitterly cold. Touring in the winter was a much different experience than touring during the warmer months. I don't think there's any place colder than a windy tarmac in January. But, right away, I knew it was going to be a fantastic experience. Dave and his band were not like crazy rock and rollers. It was very low key and almost family-like. I think a lot of that had to do with the fact that Dave's mom, Nora, was along for the ride. I absolutely fell in love with her right from the moment I met her. She was funny and charming and was just so proud of Dave. She and I became good friends right away. In fact, when the tour eventually made it through Birmingham, Alabama, and my mom got to go, they became good friends as well!

During that initial run, I think we did twenty-five shows in thirty days. It was crazy. I didn't know how Dave was physically able to go out there each night, play, and sing as he did, and then do the exact same thing night after night after night. But he did it. I think part of the reason he was able to keep up with the schedule was just how relaxed an environment everybody maintained on the plane. Again, I don't remember any wild parties. I'm sure things were going on from time to time, but you didn't see it on the plane. The plane was really just like a big living room. I made sure the guys all had food; I was the nurse; I was everything they needed me to be. Dave's mom sewed all the buttons on stage outfits when everybody needed it, so she totally fit right in and became part of the crew. I also think that people in the band may have behaved themselves a little bit more because Nora was there. I mean, you're not going to get all crazy in front of Dave's mom, you know?

Searchin' (For a Feeling)

I'm searching for a feeling deep inside
I'll find it; it's a feeling you can't hide

Many have come and gone; few have stayed
Many have taken much that wasn't theirs to claim
We're all just trying to give the most we can
Trying to work it out, and that's the plan

I'm searching for a way to plant the seed
I'll find it; it's a feeling we all need

We're children who are walking in the light
Still hoping that it all works out alright
Many have come and gone; few have stayed
Many have taken much that wasn't theirs to claim
We're all just trying to give the most we can
Trying to work it out, and that's the plan

I'm searching for a feeling deep inside
I'll find it; it's a feeling you can't hide

CHAPTER FOURTEEN

Searchin' (For a Feeling)

Back then, recording contracts usually called for two albums a year. Trying to keep this pace while maintaining the quality of *Let It Flow,* in addition to spending most of the time on the road, was basically an impossible task. Because of this, I was pretty much good for one album a year. This put you on suspension on your contract, meaning it just kept getting extended—a screwed-up deal for the artist. It's basically an expensive way for an artist to borrow money. At any rate, by the following year, 1978, it was time to come up with something new.

Once again, I opted to not use a recording studio but to do something more comfortable for me. Wally Heider's, a prominent LA studio at the time, had a well-equipped mobile recording truck. It wouldn't be a boat this time but my house at Mariposa de Oro. Since we'd worked so well together on previous albums, I brought in Ron Nevison to engineer and coproduce with me.

The house was basically a 4,800 square-foot, one-bedroom home with a 2,800 square-foot living room that had 15-foot ceilings. The living room also had a full-size Steinway grand piano. And that's where we would record my album *Mariposa de Oro*.

At that time, I'd met and started hanging out with a fellow named Jerry Williams, who is probably one of the most talented people I've ever known. He wrote "Running on Faith" that was recorded by Eric Clapton, among other things. (In fact, he wrote that one for me to record, but I didn't like it.) He also wrote Bonnie Raitt's "Real Man" and BB King's "Standing on the Edge of Love."

Jerry was born in Texas and was part American Indian. He always had a pistol with him and always wore a serape. Jerry could have been a huge artist in his own right, but he was crazier than a shithouse rat.

He was also, I should add, my coke buddy. But this guy would sit down and write two or three songs a day; they would pour out of him. He became an integral part of the album, writing or cowriting five of the songs that were eventually included on *Mariposa de Oro*. Some years later, he was diagnosed with cancer, and in true Jerry Williams style, instead of seeking treatment, I understand he bought a boat and sailed it to St. Martin in the Caribbean, where he lived his final days—I'm sure having a hell of a good time.

The band had changed by the time we cut *Mariposa de Oro*. Mike Finnigan and Jim Krueger went on to form a group with Les Dudek called DFK, but they came back to be part of the recording of the album. Jim contributed a beautiful song called "The Words," which was an ode to his favorite author, John Steinbeck.

I never had to leave during the recording, which was both good and bad. Good because it was convenient. Bad because I could indulge however I wanted to around the clock. Regular life blurred with the recording process. The Wally Heider truck was in the driveway, and I got Jerry Williams a mobile home on the property to live in since I really didn't have room at my house. That way, he and I had more time to write songs together—and also more time to do coke together. A lot of the basic tracks were done right in my living room at Mariposa.

Once we finished laying down the tracks, I was off on the road doing more shows. When it came time to finish up the album and all the mixing, I decided to move everything to Miami at Criteria Studios. It was one of the most happening studios putting out huge records. The Bee Gees were recording the soundtrack for *Saturday Night Fever* there; Clapton's

451 Ocean Boulevard and Andy Gibb's *Shadow Dancing* sessions were going on. Crosby, Stills & Nash were there as well. In true rock and roll style, I rented a house right on the water with a great view of Miami and the cruise ships. And that's where my girlfriend Cathy (who was back in the mix after I stopped seeing Leigh), Ron Nevison, and I set up house with a cook who came in every day. Miami, what a place to be. The cocaine capital of the USA. Oh, boy.

At that time, there was a small community of houses about two miles out in the ocean, built on a sandbar called Stiltsville, a fantastic spot. One day, Steven Stills, Cathy, and I got invited to someone's house out there. We, of course, didn't hesitate and jumped on their cigarette boat, where the party was in full swing. They had a couple of instruments, so Stills and I got into an impromptu jam session.

Meanwhile, when it came time to do the vocals on *Mariposa,* since Jim Krueger was no longer with the band, I needed someone who could sing the high harmonies. Ron Albert, one of the owners of Criteria, suggested a local guy they used a lot for guitar and vocals named John Sambataro. John turned out to be the perfect choice, and he's still with me to this  day. He's an excellent guitar player and singer. Gerry Beckley and Dewey Bunnell—that is, the band America—were gracious enough to come sing some harmonies on the song "It Will Make You Wonder." Graham Nash even came over to sing on "No Doubt About It."

Mariposa was never the hit I'd hoped even though I had a strong cover version of "Will You Still Love Me Tomorrow." We did a video of that song that was shot at Mariposa de Oro, and we used the house as the album cover. I had a white suit made by Jacques Bellini in New York, who was making a lot of my clothes at the time. The photographs weren't done by the label but shot by my friend Mara Magliadici. Though not a commercial success, it's one of my favorite albums that I've done.

My friend Mara.

Johnny Sambataro is an acclaimed singer, songwriter, and guitar player, and has played and toured with Dave for over forty years.

He and Dave are close friends.

Johnny Sambataro:
By 1978, I was basically on the map as an on-call studio singer and player at Criteria near where I lived in Miami. That year I was working on Andy Gibb's album Shadow Dancing *when Dave Mason booked the studio*

to work on his next album, Mariposa De Oro. *I didn't know a ton about Dave,* but what I knew, I loved. I was a big Traffic fan, and in 1971 while I was going to college in Boston, his first solo album Alone Together *was a gamechanger for me.* My guitar-player friends and I would sit there playing that album over and over, trying to figure out all of the different and brilliant tunings he used. I only knew how to tune the guitar one way, the standard way my dad taught me when I was eight years old. But Dave was just doing so much. I knew nothing about tuning a half step down, tuning the E string to D or tuning both E strings down to D or tuning to an EE court in the first position. Interestingly, the Bee Gees were actually doing a lot of that. Barry Gibb had a knack for writing songs in multiple tunings, so I was starting to learn those things when I first met Dave.

Typically, with Andy, we would work the day shift from 10 in the morning until about 6 PM or so. Dave would roll in about 9 o'clock at night and work until 4 AM. So, I never saw him, but I knew he was there. There was always a *buzz* when somebody like Dave Mason was working at Criteria. People would linger more than they did usually, just wanting to get a glimpse of him or watch him work if it were possible. Having Dave Mason there was a big deal.

One night, while I was at home, I got a call from Ron Albert. He told me that Dave was looking for a background singer and that my name came up. He wanted to get in touch with me, and Ron asked if it was OK if he gave Dave my number. I told him of course, but then a minute later I guess Dave walked in the room and took the phone from Ron and simply said to me, "Can you come in tonight at about 11 o'clock?"

"Absolutely," I told him.

When I got to the studio, engineer Ron Nevison put a track up and told me what they were looking for. Then, all of a sudden, Graham Nash walked in, and Ron asked me if I would mind singing with Graham on the track. Was he kidding? I was beyond honored. Crosby, Stills & Nash had been in the studio at that same time. Evidently, things had gone south in their sessions just several hours earlier. David Crosby and Stephen Stills had had a big fight, and Crosby left the sessions to hop on a plane back to Los Angeles. Graham Nash hung around, and it's a good thing that he did. Graham was terrific. He made me feel comfortable, and he liked what I was doing.

After we finished Dave's session, a few nights later, Dave, Andy Gibb, and I did background vocals on the abandoned CSN project that had now morphed into a Stephen Stills solo record called Thoroughfare Gap. *Throughout the next couple* of weeks, Dave and I were hanging out more and more. Things were getting kind of strange in the Andy Gibb camp. For reasons I'm still not sure about, Andy's team *didn't want me playing guitar in his touring band. They loved what I was doing in the studio, but there was some political situation about having me on the road. I'm not sure if it was a problem with other band members or whatever, but it was an issue.*

Dave picked up on the weirdness, and one night, he and I had a conversation. He told me he found it uncomfortable and strange and that I should watch myself. He also said he would love to have me in his band touring the Mariposa *album later in the year. "I'll give you a call," he said. I thought it was just small talk that artists did but then never followed up on.*

But then, in early May, he called me and invited me to come live in his house. "We're going to start rehearsing soon," he said, "and you can get acclimated with the rest of the band and what we want to do."

At that time, my wife was pregnant, and our son Jason was about two years old. My wife and I had long conversations about whether it was the right thing to do. In the end, we decided it would be OK. The money was going to be really good, and Dave was really showing faith in me. He really had no idea how I played guitar. He had hired me to be a singer, but he had a sense about me; he trusted me, and that meant a lot. My wife and I both decided it was the right thing to do, and even though I would be gone for months, we would figure it out.

So off I went to Malibu, California. Dave really took me under his wing and started teaching me all of those weird and wonderful tunings that I had listened to years earlier. I was pinching myself. Of all the guitar players he knew, he picked me. I hadn't been on the road before, really. I had played a little bit with Andy, but I had never left home. I would just do one-off shows with him.

Once we hit the road, the audiences were amazing, and it blew my mind just how much people loved Dave Mason. His fans represented this huge cross section of people. There were lots of people from the old Traffic days and then plenty of teenagers who had just become familiar with "We Just Disagree" and the new album.

I won't lie; there was a lot of excess on the road in terms of drinking and cocaine, but nothing ever got out of control. Having our own plane meant that we had our own little environment contained to ourselves, which was nice. In late August, as my birthday approached, I realized that we were going to be playing in Miami not too far from where I grew up. Dave had an idea. "Why don't you tell your wife to pack a bag and bring your son out for the rest of the tour? I think it would be good for both of you." It was a very generous offer, and we jumped at the chance. To me, that really summed up what Dave Mason was all about. He was a rock 'n' roller but he also had this sense about the importance of family. He knew my apprehension of having a pregnant wife at home and wanted to accommodate it.

But he even went one step further.

Certain cities for us became "hub" cities. That is, we might base ourselves in Chicago and then fly out to surrounding cities to do gigs but then come back to Chicago after the show. We were booked at the beautiful Ritz Carlton hotel there for about a week or two. The guys in the band were wonderful when it came to helping us look after our son Jason. They loved him, and Jason loved them right back. One day our bass player, a wonderful guy named Gerald Johnson, said to me, "Why don't you take your wife out to breakfast? There's a great café close to the hotel, and it will give you two a chance to be alone. I'll watch Jason for you." We thought that was a great idea. But when Gerald came to our room, he was blown away. "You two have a suite?" he asked incredulously.

We didn't know what to say. We had no idea what kind of rooms the other band members had, and to be honest, in every city we went to, we had a large suite. So, my wife went to the tour manager, Richie Fernandez. She asked about the rooms and what was going on. He said to her, "I'll tell you one time, but please don't repeat this. Dave has been giving you his suite every night. He takes the room that would've been assigned to you. The smaller room. He just wants you to be comfortable since you have a child and another one on the way."

I couldn't believe it. Neither could my wife. Over the years, David and I have worked together so many times, and occasionally we butt heads or argue or do the things that musicians do with each other. But whenever I think back to when I found out what he was doing on the road with the suites, I can never stay mad at Dave for long. I can simply never forget the fact that he was doing that and not even telling us.

Jason is forty-three now, and he's in touch with Dave. I still tour with Dave, I stay at his house, I jam with him, I hear stories, I tell stories, and I am very happy I'm in his world. I love his wife Winifred. They are family. Is Dave the easiest guy to work with or get along with? He's not. But you know what? He's Dave Mason. Artists can be tough sometimes, and he and I always manage to work it out. I've had a wonderful career playing on so many sessions with everybody from Eric Clapton to Meatloaf, to touring as a lead member of Firefall and many other things. But playing guitar with Dave Mason is something I will always look at as the job that helped establish me as a touring musician. The chance to play and learn from such a masterful, expressive, and talented artist as Dave Mason is something I will always be truly thankful for.

Maybe

Maybe I can love you, maybe be your friend
Maybe I can help you, your troubles to mend
Maybe sing a song for you, that's what I know best to do
Anything you want me to I'll be
Anything you want me to I'll be

Maybe we'll be strangers till our dying day
Maybe then we'll understand what we had to say
Maybe when we've closed the door on all that's negative in thought
Any way you want it, it can be
Any way you want it, it can be

Lift your head now; tears you've shed are all ignored
Take a hand and make a stand against all wars
Are you dreaming or just scheming for reward
Life's illusions are misleading
It's so good to be here breathing

Maybe I can love you, maybe be your friend
Maybe I can help you, your troubles to mend
Maybe sing a song for you, that's what I know best to do
Any way you want it, it can be

CHAPTER FIFTEEN

Maybe

Mariposa was finished, and I headed back to California. I'd loved what Sambataro had been doing on the *Mariposa* sessions and invited him to be part of the band. Johnny turned up at my house with a bunch of guitars. "What are you doing with all those guitars? You're a singer!" After playing with him a while, I realized that, in addition to being a damn fine singer, he was a hell of a great guitar player too.

The production for the tour was being handled by a company called Showco, which was based out of Dallas, Texas. So off we all went to Dallas for two weeks, where we rehearsed the upcoming tour. We ended up having several outstanding shows, including the largest audience I've ever played to, at Cal Jam II, which had over 300,000 people. I went to Santa Monica Airport, having been up all night, and caught a helicopter to the site at Ontario Speedway, California, for a morning show. Carlos Santana was also on the bill that day, and he and I had a chance to jam together during the set. There are too many shows for me to remember over the course of my career, but Cal Jam is always one that will stand out.

We did a similar festival that summer up in Canada and then, near the end of the summer, went out to Belmont Racetrack on Long Island. It was the day the racehorse Affirm won the Triple Crown. It had been decided it would be a nice idea to put on a concert after the race. It was the first time they'd done one. In their minds, it might be four or five thousand people who would turn up. By the time we hit the stage, there were 30,000 people out there. There were people sitting in trees and

definitely not enough porta potties to go around. Interestingly enough, I still have an old board mix of that show. Perhaps one day I'll release it.

I wasn't at home much. My relationship with my ex-wife Lorraine was rocky. I was married to my music, and as a result, I hardly ever got to see True. So, when he was eight years old, he started coming out on the road with me. Those were moments that I still treasure today. He loved flying on the plane; the band and crew loved him and always kept him entertained if I was busy.

And yet, it was still tough. Being a creative artist requires a deep passion for what you do—not unlike being an explorer who is always searching for new horizons. Neither of these professions is ideally suited for a traditional family, at least certainly not for me. So True went to live with my sister Val and her two children in San Diego. Lorraine simply was not fit at that point to be looking after children. She had some bad habits (as did I), and so it was good that Val was able to step in.

After my relationships with Cathy and Leigh and several others ran their collective courses, I got married to a woman named Dana. On November 11, 1980, my second child, Danielle, was born in Santa Monica, weighing just over six pounds. I was there to cut the cord. Not that many hours later, we all went home to Malibu and settled in with our bundle of joy. And she really was. Many hours of my day were spent with her sleeping right on my chest. From her first breath of life, I was not only there but in love. And I still am to this day.

That said, my relationship with my daughter today is, sadly, estranged. I am the first to admit I wasn't present as a father much past those first few months. Dana and I then separated shortly after our marriage. Though we had joint custody of Danielle, there were times when Dana made it difficult for me to see her. It wasn't until she was five or so that I actually started a relationship with her, in earnest, at Sea World in San Pedro, of all places, where I thought I'd scored some major points at the ring toss when I won her a huge teddy bear. I have spent every day since trying to win her love back. While I'm not proud that I failed in my role as a father in her early years, I do find some solace that the moment I knew better, I did better.

Addiction is a rocky road and one that I know well. Danielle does too, unfortunately. I've given my best in the face of what I firmly believe is a choice, and to push it off as simply a disease doesn't sit with me. To classify it as such is a way of removing any personal responsibility. The abyss of addiction is brutal for everyone involved, whether in the throes of it, on the periphery, or a direct witness to it. I'd long thought I could provide wise counsel for my daughter, and I've spent many years thinking my love for her could pull her through her own demons. Alas, as anyone who has dealt with addiction knows, you can't help someone who is in the grips of it unless they're willing and ready. It must be an internal shift. Following my last visit with Danielle, I'm happy to say things between us seem to be healing, which couldn't make a father happier.

Up until I lived in Mariposa de Oro, I'd rented houses. That was the first home I'd ever owned. The timing wasn't optimal for making such a big purchase because there was a switch in musical tastes that cut directly into my market. Punk rock had exploded out of London and was now morphing into New Wave. My brand of music wasn't as popular, and while I was still touring, it wasn't the high-profile, fat-paycheck arena shows I'd known. Now we were playing theaters, at best, and barrooms and the like more often.

I did television appearances like *American Bandstand* with Dick Clark and *The Late Show with David Letterman*. I branched out and did a film, *Skate Town,* for which I wrote and performed the title track. I'm on

screen for such a short cameo that if you blink, you'll miss me. But the experience had bigger takeaways, one being my friendship with Patrick Swayze. It was his first film, and after it wrapped, we stayed in touch. Some years later, after I'd left California and was living in Chicago, while Patrick was visiting Chicago after his filming of *Dirty Dancing*, he came over to my apartment on Lake Shore Drive. My girlfriend at the time was drooling all over him (but what woman wasn't during that time?). One of the big clubs in Chicago was The Limelight. It was like the one in New York except it wasn't in a church, but in a large building with two or three levels. It was one of the oldest buildings in Chicago, built in 1892 after the great Chicago fire by architect Henry Ives Cobb. Some say it's haunted, but in my mind, it was full of life. Patrick kept a motorbike in Chicago and arrived at my place with it. I hopped on the back, and away we went. While enjoying a cocktail in the VIP room and surveying the scene, he leaned over and said, "God, I'd love to dance, but with the movie out, I just don't know." I responded, "Who gives a shit, man? Go dance if you want to dance!" He did, and it caused quite a stir. We stayed out all night and finished up at Kingston Mines, a great blues club run by a guy named Doc who wore the cool Coke-bottle eyeglasses. Patrick was catching a plane that morning, and when we got back to my place well after the sun was up, he said, "I need to get thirty minutes of sleep." He did, and left for his flight later that morning. And that's the last I ever saw of Patrick Swayze.

This era had its challenges. I mean, all eras do, but this one was especially taxing. I was still staying busy, but it wasn't the heyday of the 1970s. I wasn't playing Madison Square Garden and the likes anymore. When you've played to 300,000 and "all the right places," it's quite an adjustment to accept a new reality. I was fretting about this professional scenario, and to put things even more in perspective, along came a bigger and even more painful reality that hit me square in the face.

Life, as it will do, threw me a curveball when my mother got sick. That changed everything. She was a force of nature. She could, by sheer will and effort, turn tears into laughter, despair into hope. She was able to give comfort and be my best friend. She dispensed constant encouragement to me as a young boy on my way to manhood. She accomplished this in a seemingly effortless way, while at the same time doing the laundry, cooking dinner, and cleaning the house. On the other hand, one did not want to cross her or get on the wrong side of her. The heavens would open up and punishment was delivered rather swiftly, usually in the form of a severe tongue lashing, sometimes worse.

She had been a central part of my life. This is the woman, after all, who took money out of the till at the candy store to buy me my first guitar. She was trustworthy and dependable, totally no-nonsense, not to mention hilarious and about as far away from "show business" as they come, though she went out on tour with me many, many times. She became very close with my friend Mara, and they would go shopping and out to lunches and dinners together. Mom carried a silver cigarette case that my father was given for saving a boy from drowning in Wales. While waiting in line to see some movie in Westwood, Mara tells me my mother proceeded to pull a joint out of said cigarette case and fire it up. I loved her very much.

So when she was diagnosed with cancer, I was devastated.

I was still out doing concerts, so Mom moved from her Santa Monica apartment to stay with my sister in San Diego to start treatment. They had her on the usual treatments, chemotherapy and such, yet it was having no positive effect. Her tumor was too large, so they had to remove it surgically.

I drove from Malibu down to La Jolla to be with her the day after her surgery. I was met by the doctor who performed the operation. He proceeded to tell me they couldn't remove the tumor because it was too close to her heart, and would I mind telling her, "When you cut somebody open with cancer and you don't remove it all, it spreads like wildfire"? This doctor just told me I had to go inform my mother that she was going to die. I didn't know whether to break down and cry or strangle him right then and there.

In my mind, there is such honor in the duty of a son to his mother. While I'm not sure delivering the news of this death sentence was a son's duty, what was I supposed to do?

I walked into her room and gave her the information the doctor relayed to me. She just looked at me and said, "I know."

My mother was then moved back to my sister's house in San Diego. She was bedridden at this point, and whilst visiting her one sunny southern California day, she turned to me with a desperate look in her eyes and said, "You have to get me out of here." It was bad enough that the house was directly under the takeoff flight path of the San Diego airport, but evidently her daughter (my sister), who had become a bad alcoholic by that point, was making things intolerable. I immediately called an ambulance service and had my mother driven to my house in Malibu. I had to keep working because I had no medical insurance. My mother was dying, so everything to me was very black and white. I had no time for any bullshit from anybody, no time for ifs, ands, or buts. She brought me into this world, and it was my moral obligation to help her leave it in the most dignified manner possible. Mom was wasting away, and her motor senses were waning. One afternoon, in the midst of her literally dying before my eyes, I was holding her hand by her bed. I asked her if she was afraid of dying. She paused for a moment, then said, "No, but I am afraid of the loneliness of dying." I squeezed her hand and promised her I'd be right there with her.

Yet she wasn't one to give up. Maybe that's where I get my stubborn, steadfast resolve. I located a specialist in Beverly Hills with the hope of providing her with a Brompton's mixture, which was sometimes used in hospice for advanced cancer patients: morphine, THC, and cocaine.

"Right now, we're having a hard time getting our hands on cocaine," the doctor said. Well, wasn't this ironic?

"I can make a call for you," I assured him.

But nothing transpired. There were no more treatments. They thought they could give her back her speech, which she had recently lost. But in doing so, this would also wake her up to her pain. I hired full-time nurses, day and night.

My home in Serra Retreat Malibu, Mariposa De Oro, was a large, very beautiful Moorish-style home. To get a visual take on the house, it appears in the movie *Father of the Bride* in a scene where Steve Martin is being chased by Dobermans. This magnificent house was said to be built on Native American Indian burial grounds. I'm not a religious man, but I *am* spiritually inclined. The days preceding Mom's death, our cat disappeared, birds were literally dashing themselves into the windows, and wisps of things in my peripheral vision were flying around in my large living room. I can only account for these occurrences as spirits. Death has a way of taking up the whole house when it's on the doorstep.

The evening before my mother passed away, I went out to dinner at a local Malibu Italian restaurant with my dear pal Dan Haggerty. Mr. Grizzly Adams himself. We'd been friends for some time, and I needed to take my mind off things for a couple of hours; I needed a break. We got shown to a very nice booth, and who's next to us? Don Rickles! He was sitting with his whole family and hurling wisecracks at Dan from the minute we sat down and one or two at me. He had no idea how much I needed to laugh like that.

When I got home later that night, the nurse greeted me at the door. "It's just about that time," she said to me.

My sister was there, too, but she was making things hard for everyone. She was sitting at the foot of her bed, saying to my mom, "You're leaving me, how dare you go dying." My sister's drinking problem was manifesting itself at this horrible moment. I finally had to physically pull her out of the room to quiet her down so my mom could be at peace. The nurse had told us that the sense of hearing is the last thing to go. I wanted my mom's last moments to be peaceful. Then the nurse and I held Mom's hands until she took her last breath.

My best friend and most diehard supporter was gone. Part of me felt like I died, too. I practically collapsed under the weight of it all and

was so very tired, physically, emotionally, and spiritually. I went to lie down on the chaise in the kitchen while the nurse called the medics and the police. While lying there falling asleep, I saw three rushes of purple light come at me followed by a very clear vision of Mom's face. She looked as if she had just come from the hairdresser, smiling and as perfect as ever. Say what you will, but I know I got to see my mom's soul leave the room. I knew everything was fine, and I fell asleep.

I hosted Mom's memorial service at a little church in Santa Monica and invited all the people that she had touched. Stephen Stills came. Graham Nash sang "Teach Your Children." I sang her favorite song of mine, "Maybe." And then Mike Finnigan got up there and proceeded to rock that little church with his version of "Going to a Higher Ground." Mom would have loved it. And hopefully did.

To top everything off, I was planning on taking Mom's ashes back to England, to place them next to my father's grave in Worcester. The morning I was to leave, I went to wake up my tour manager, who was staying with me, so he could take me to the airport. The problem was, he wouldn't wake up, and he was starting to get a noticeable bluish hue to his skin. He was falling into a coma. Looking back, why I thought to call Dan Haggerty and not the paramedics, I do not know. I called them right after, but Dan came to the house immediately and proceeded to give him mouth to mouth until the paramedics came. What the hell was going on? It turned out that track marks were found on his body—between his toes, fingers, everywhere that was not visible. He had worked with me for a number of years, and I had no idea he was using heroin. Somehow, he pulled through, but it rattled me.

In just a matter of months after losing Mom, I would also lose that beautiful Malibu house, along with almost everything else I owned and cared about. It was the music that saved me. The only thing I could do was take my ass back out on the road to sing for my supper and everything else that needed to be paid for. And then some.

Mike Finnigan is an acclaimed keyboard, organ player, and singer. He was a member of Dave's band in the 1970s and they remained friends until Mike's death in 2021.

Mike Finnigan:

Dave Mason's touring band, 1970s, is one of the greatest outfits I've ever been a part of. The things we did each night onstage were just so memorable, not just for me, but I'm sure for everybody in the band. I just loved Dave's stuff leading up to that. I think he had always had good bands because he seemed to appreciate the fact that surrounding yourself with decent players made you look good. He and I connected well at the audition, and then he offered me the job and we just hit the ground running.

Not many artists kept the schedule in terms of performances that Dave Mason did in the 1970s. Colleges, especially, embraced him as a touring act, and we played hundreds of college shows. It was just something about the kind of concert that Dave Mason gave that appealed to college-age kids. I think because his shows included so many different kinds of music. You got rock 'n' roll, you got rhythm and blues, you got blues, you got some folk—it was just a great assortment of things that everybody likes. College kids were so open to stuff like that, and also a lot of the jamming that Dave Mason shows always featured.

There are guys at Dave's level that have massive egos, and they want you to stay in your place as a band member. Dave was the exact opposite. Again, his whole thing was, get the right guys and let them do the right things. Let everybody stretch, let everybody explore, and give people room to perform and grow.

I loved singing, and Dave liked my voice, so I always had a spot in the show where I could sing lead. That was always fun. But all of the guys got their turns to show off a little bit onstage. Was there a lot of excess on the road? For sure. We did drugs. There was a lot of cocaine, booze, and some other things as well. But we always showed up to play. The show always mattered most. We might share a joint or something before going on stage, but the shows were never jeopardized by other things that were going on. Today, I'm a recovering alcoholic. I haven't had a drink in thirty-three years, but back then was a different story. And my good buddy Jim Krueger was truly addicted to alcohol. In the end, it wound up killing him, taking him from us at far too young an age.

But on the road in the '70s, I have to say there really wasn't too much drama; we all got along great in the band, and we all worked hard to make all of those shows the best they could be. And there were some massive shows. I mean, we got to play with Elton John; we performed in front of about 300,000 people at Cal Jam II. Dave Mason was a major act, and so we were headlining all over the place, or at least coheadlining with major artists. There was very little we wanted for.

I also loved Dave's mom. Nora was on the road with us from time to time. Talk about a cool lady. If joints were going around on our little private plane, she would happily take a hit off of one. She would tell us stories about what Dave was like growing up, and everybody from the crew to the fans just thought she was amazing. How many rock stars bring their mom on the road like that? When she passed away, I sang at her funeral, which is one of the hardest things I ever had to do. I just kept looking up at the ceiling at this little church in Santa Monica, thinking to myself, "Nora, I sure hope you can hear this. Because things just won't be the same down here without you."

The Lonely One

There've been moments of despair, there've been times I couldn't care
I was the lonely one
Then you showed myself to me, and I found I needn't be
Another lonely one

Running in the wilderness and dreaming in the sun
And crying to the sky at night for God's eternal son

Through the truth and through the lies, there is really no disguise
To hide the lonely ones
You can find them on a card being matched with other hearts
The really lonely ones

Running in the wilderness and dreaming in the sun
And crying to the sky at night for God's eternal son

Inside your rooms, behind your wall
I see your face, you know I hear your call
Is this some madness that's been left unchecked
Or will there always be just promises?

Running in the wilderness and dreaming in the sun
And crying to the sky at night for God's eternal son

There are men that hold the key to set everybody free
But they are lonely ones
And if the day should come when they all can work as one
There'll be a destiny, yes I know

Running in the wilderness and dreaming in the sun
Cryin' to the sky at night for God's eternal son, yeah, yeah . . .

CHAPTER SIXTEEN

The Lonely One

My last album for Columbia, and really my last album for a major label, was *Old Crest on a New Wave*. Some of the old band was back together during the recording of the album: Jim Krueger on vocals and guitar, Rick Jaeger on drums, Mike Finnigan on keyboards and vocals. I'd brought in Joe Wissert to produce the album. He'd been with Columbia for a number of years. One of the albums he'd produced was Boz Skaggs's *Silk Degrees*. I was hoping some of his magic would rub off for my new album. But looking back on it now, there really wasn't anything strong enough on it for a single, and I was battling what at that time was called new wave music. That's what inspired the title, and that's why there's a picture of a baby wearing boxing gloves on the cover—which, by the way, isn't me. There are four different colors of that album jacket, and any way you find it, Dave Mason wasn't in the public favor so much for this album.

The most memorable session from *Old Crest on a New Wave* was having Michael Jackson sing on a song called "Save Me." When it got to doing vocals on the song, I needed some high harmonies. It just happened that Michael Jackson was recording *Off the Wall* with Quincy Jones in the next studio. It was just too tempting not to ask him. I walked over to the other studio, and Michael happened to be standing in the doorway of the control room. They were on a break, so I introduced myself and asked if he would sing the high parts. He paused for a minute and looked at me. "You know, when I was twelve years old, I was doing a TV special with Diana Ross. At the end of the show, Diana and The Jackson Five sang your song 'Feelin' Alright?' So, yes, absolutely. Of course, I'll come sing." He ended up doing more than just the little high harmony part I needed. He got into it and started dancing and throwing in more parts than I'd asked for and more than I ever expected him to do.

That album, when it was finished, was not only a Dave Mason album, but also a Joe Wissert production, so I thought Columbia would go all-out on promotion. Not to be. They let it die, and it was the last album I made for Columbia and the last album Joe Wissert ever produced for them.

The question—a question I was awfully familiar with—became again: Now what?

My marriage with Dana had fallen apart, as I said. One day, I went to see David Baxter, a good friend and sweet spirit who was living on Ron Popeil's boat in Marina del Rey. I thought he was there by himself, but when I arrived, I was met on board by not only David, but also by this gorgeous blond beauty, Pam. I was smitten at first sight. It effectively ended my marriage with Dana, which led to me coming back to Mariposa one day to find every stick of furniture gone.

I was getting financially strapped again and refinanced Mariposa at a ludicrous interest rate. I had to go back on the road, but you have to understand, to go out with a full band and production is an extremely expensive proposition. What I'd earn for myself wasn't going to be enough to support the lifestyle I was leading. The only way to make money was to cut my tour overhead dramatically. And what was the solution? An acoustic show. It was going to be a big gamble; artists like me weren't doing that. But necessity being the mother of invention, Jim Krueger and I hit the road as a duo.

It wasn't really fun for me because I couldn't play electric lead guitar, and I love, after all, playing electric. It is the very reason I got into the music game itself. Jim Krueger was an awesome guitar player, one of the best I've ever played with. And though we had many fine moments, it was unfulfilling for me artistically. I was left with rhythm guitar and singing, which didn't excite me. We played every venue, from theaters to upholstered sewers, for more than two years. And even though I was at first apprehensive, the audiences were appreciative. What it did show was the old adage in the music business that it's all about the song, the song, the song. And even though I had misgivings about this tour, I did have songs, and this is what really kept the audiences coming to see what essentially was just two people on stage.

Eventually, a few years later, there would be a successful TV show called *Unplugged*. I guess we saw it coming, but we were just a bit early for the boat. The only surviving testimonial to what Jim and I were doing is a DVD we made called *Dave Mason Live at Perkins Palace*. I am still waiting to see the royalties from it.

None of this saved me from losing my house. I ended up giving it to Scott Lavin, heir to Alberto Culver, who wanted to be in the music business and very much wanted to help me. Instead of my beautiful house going back to the bank, Scott took it over in trade for the time he'd spent helping me with my business. Scott had more than enough money

as a trust fund baby; he could have helped me keep the house. Instead, he just assumed the debt and took the house. I was too in the hole and didn't know what else to do. The relationship didn't end well. A year or two later, I was in Chicago at a hotel while on tour, and out of the blue I got a phone call from Scott. How he knew I was there I have no clue, but I was still really mad in the sense I'd felt taken advantage of. He was calling to make amends and apologize, but I was still too angry and hung up the phone on him. It was not long after that that I heard through the grapevine that, sadly, he'd overdosed. Drugs don't care how much money or privilege you may or may not have.

Before I let Mariposa go, I decided to throw a big party along with Cheech Marin, a friend I'd gotten to know along the way while living in Malibu. Despite it being an outrageous affair, it was, for me, one of the more depressing nights of my life. For anyone who came to it, however, it was a gala event. I hired retired police officers for security because so many celebrities were coming. It was packed and star-studded, but I was so out of it I didn't even know who all was there. I do remember Mick Fleetwood and Ryan O'Neill. I also recall that, at some point in the evening when I wanted to escape to my bedroom, I found Stevie Nicks and a friend of hers sitting in my closet. I regret screaming at her to get the fuck out of my house. She still won't speak to me to this day. And only afterward did I find out Keith Richards and some of the other Stones came down from the Playboy Mansion to party with us.

After I lost Mariposa, Pam and I moved into the Marina del Ray City Club, where someone who would become a good friend lived: Ed Silvers. Ed was one of the heads of Warner Chappell music and had courted me at one point to acquire my music publishing. My career was at somewhat of a standstill, and as it happened, Ed was helping his friend Leon Russell organize his publishing, which was in some disarray. Ed started throwing around the idea of a super group with me, Leon, and perhaps one other performer. I don't remember exactly how, but Gary Wright became part of the group. That was cool with me since I had known Gary since his days with his band Spooky Tooth over in England. They were on Island Records and were managed by Chris Blackwell. Ed owned the song "Time Is on My Side" and another song he was eager to record, "Just Another Flash in Japan."

The three of us didn't really have any new material, so it was decided that Ed, Gary, and I would move near Leon's home in Hendersonville, Tennessee, where he had a recording studio, and start coming up with material for an album. Ed, Gary, Pam, and I rented a house overlooking a

(L-R): Gary Wright, me, Rocky Dzidzornu, and Leon Russell at Leon's house in Tennessee.

lake. We cut the track for "Time Is On My Side," which I thought was a perfect song for Leon. His distinct voice and piano playing gave it a very different interpretation from the Stones' version. We tried to come up with original material, but for whatever reason, we came up empty. No one was really keen on singing "Flash in Japan." It was a great idea to put the three of us together, but it never really jelled between us. I think it was partly because it was a contrived concept rather than something that was more organic in its inception. For whatever reason, Mason, Russell & Wright vanished into the annuls of rock and roll history.

Ed Silvers was also an avid sailor and owned a beautiful forty-eight-foot Swan sailing boat named *Into The Mystic*. He eventually retired from the music business and moved to Virgin Gorda in the British Virgin Islands. It was a great little house in Leverick Bay overlooking Necker Island, which is Sir Richard Branson's Getaway. I have some wonderful memories with Ed at his home there and out sailing on his boat.

Two Hearts

What kind of game are you playing, playing with my heart
Lying to yourself if you think we could ever stay apart
You can't hide the way you feel for me
Your foolish pride and your insecurity
There'll come a day filled with retribution
You're gonna find out there's only one solution

Two hearts, searching for affection
Two hearts, in the right direction
Two hearts, somethings on the mind of two hearts
You know love is gonna find two hearts

Don't run away 'cause you're too scared to be alone
You're gonna do something foolish out there on your own
You're gonna find out it ain't so easy
Maybe you'll understand I gave so freely
You're gonna lose a friendship and a lover
And then it's gonna be too late to rediscover

Two hearts searching for affection
Two hearts in the right direction
Two hearts, something's on the mind of two hearts
You know love is gonna find two hearts

CHAPTER SEVENTEEN

Two Hearts

In the late 1980s, long after I'd lost everything at Mariposa, a very gracious Mick Fleetwood let me and Pam use his guest house for a number of months at his home in Malibu, affectionately called The Blue Whale. We passed a lot of time playing *Trivial Pursuit*. As an artist, I was dead. For a minute, I was managed by Helen Reddy's husband, Jeff Wald, who was a big deal, but to no avail. I was entering into one of the lowest chapters of my life. There was a period when I wasn't even picking up a guitar to play, and I quit writing. It was a dark five or so years.

Pam

I did, however, manage to make an album called *Some Assembly Required* for an independent label. I practically have to be reminded I even made this album. I'd totally lost heart in my work and in my life, and it was really a matter of just going through the motions. I mean, what else was I going to do? There was no marketing or promotion, and the album didn't do anything. It isn't surprising, given that I didn't even care about it or, for that matter, anything else.

There I was, renting houses again, and back on the road even more, but without a home base to care about. And I had no record label. The excesses of the '70s, coupled with the downshift in demand for my concerts and records, bankrupted me emotionally as well as financially. For the first time in my musical career, I experienced a decline from which I wouldn't easily bounce back.

In about 1987, Pam and I relocated to Laguna Beach, California. Lee Abrams and Denny Somack were radio executives who formed a small label that was distributed by MCA. Since radio was an important part of getting music heard, it felt like a great opportunity to get involved with these people. We signed a contract and then set about doing a new record called *Two Hearts*. I was going to produce it myself with an engineer I'd met named Jimmy Hotz, who was proficient in the new techno world we were moving into. I decided we'd move in that direction, meaning there were no live drums or bass; rather, we would program those sounds. We went to record that project, strangely enough, in a place I'd live a few decades in the future, Carson City, Nevada, in a studio called Granny's House. It was the perfect place to get away from the distractions of the LA scene and everything down there. It had excellent guest quarters, a full kitchen with cooks, and all the makings of a place to focus on the work at hand.

I thought I'd reach out to Steve Winwood while doing that album. I had what I thought was a cool song, "Two Hearts." Surprisingly enough, he said he would do it, so I went to Nashville, where he sang the harmony parts.

I had one other song I thought was a strong contender for a single, a duet with Phoebe Snow called "The Dreams I Dream." I had known Phoebe since my days at the Chateau Marmont. We'd been friends for a long time, and I'd played on her first album, *Poetry Man*. The song was strong enough to warrant a video, but not just any old MTV video. Jack Kellman, whom I was working with; my longtime dear friend Terry Cohen; our film crew; Pam; Phoebe, and I all boarded a plane and set off for Jamaica. We had a lot of fun there, shot a great video, and of course smoked a lot of ganja. While there, I got an invitation from Paul McCartney, who happened to be staying on the island with his family, and it was nice to reunite with him.

I had high hopes for the album. It didn't click. Yep, you know what's next: I'm on the road—again. The label that Lee and Danny started didn't really take off. I like Lee Abrams a lot but feel some of his decisions have made getting music on terrestrial radio somewhat more difficult. Up until that time, you had AM and FM radio and DJs. Lee Abrams was instrumental in how radio would become formatted, which, in my mind, led to the loss of great DJs and hearing new music from classic rock artists like me. He went on to help start and become the head of XM radio.

Paul Shaker is an art dealer who is a close friend and former roommate of Dave's.

Paul Shaker:
I got to know Dave when he was living in Laguna in 1985. He was kind of at a strange point in his life and career. I know that his big heyday professionally had passed him by, but he was still playing a lot and putting on great shows. He would perform at a local place called The Sandpiper. I loved watching him play. It was such a casual place, I just walked up to him one night and started talking.

I became good friends with him and his then-girlfriend Pam. About six months later, we all packed up and found a place in a canyon out in Thousand Oaks, a big,

beautiful house, and that's when he was recording the album which became Two Hearts. *I was in the gemstone business back then, flying back and forth to Europe all the time. In fact, I lent him those heart-shaped diamonds that were photographed for the cover of the album.*

You just never knew what was going to happen with Dave. There were always interesting characters hanging around back then: musicians, actors, and other people he knew from over the years. But there was one event that I remember distinctly that really impressed me. Probably because it illustrated just how Dave was all about the music and not really impressed by any kind of celebrity.

I was over in Spain for work, and I met a girl. We spent the night partying pretty hard, and, as it turned out, we would be flying back to the United States on the same flight. We basically stayed up all night, talked together the whole plane flight back, then said goodbye to each other once we landed back in Los Angeles. I got back to the house and was completely exhausted, having been up at that point for a long time and really hitting it kind of hard.

The second I got back, Pam said that I needed to go out with her and Dave that night. But I said to her, "I have to crash. I'm really dead." But she would not have any of it. She insisted, and so the two of them practically dragged me to a tiny club somewhere out in Calabasas. It was a benefit show that was happening for, I believe, a roadie who had been injured in a car accident. Dave, as he often did, was donating his time to help somebody out. He was always very charitable with his talent.

I entered the club that night, and who was he playing with? David Crosby, Stephen Stills, Jackson Browne, and Roy Orbison. Eddie Van Halen was sitting in the front row along with some other local musical luminaries. I couldn't believe it. Roy Orbison? One of the absolute living legends of the time. I was backstage with Dave, and he just shrugged his shoulders. No big deal. And he just killed it that night. Incredibly, as I was leaving, I saw the girl from Spain I'd flown back with! Somehow or another, someone brought her to the same show.

Dave soon moved to Chicago where he started the next chapter of his life, but living with him in that big house in the canyon was a real experience. I got to watch, up close and personal, what his creative process was like, both playing live and working in the home studio he had built. David is a dedicated craftsman. A true artist who is all about the music.

Jack Kellman is a friend of Dave's from the 1970s, and they remain close friends to this day.

Jack Kellman:
I'll always remember how I met Dave Mason. David had just made Alone Together, *an album that really established him as a great singer/songwriter. It made a lot of noise, as they say. I was managing Minnie Riperton, and we were recording her new album at the Record Plant in Los Angeles. Stevie Wonder was producing, and there was lots of crazy stuff going on. I mean, we were in one studio, John Lennon and Phil Spector were in the room next to us, and then Quincy Jones was in the next room—just an amazing time. So, I'm in the bathroom, and in comes my friend Terry Cohen. He says, "Dave Mason is on the hunt, and I thought you might be able to help him out." I knew what he was talking about; cocaine was what everybody wanted. And then Dave appeared from right behind Terry and said, "Hey, there. You got a toot?"*

We became friends right away, and I loved him. I thought he was a very talented and funny guy. But we would not start working together for a long time. I'm a Chicago guy, and I eventually went back home to take care of myself and stop some of the habits that I had developed in Los Angeles in the 1970s. When Dave moved to Chicago in the mid-1980s, we reconnected.

David signed with MCA records when Irving Azoff was president, and I was good friends with Irving. Dave asked me to be his manager, I think in the hopes that I could create a good relationship for him at the label and also help him break the album he was working on, which became Two Hearts. *Really great record. I* remember he told me we had to *fly down* to Nashville because somehow or another, he had arranged for Steve Winwood to play on one song. I knew a little bit of the history of those guys: I knew that there had been a lot of tension in Traffic and what had happened to Dave years earlier when they forced him out of the band. It didn't surprise me that the mood was kind of tense in the studio. You could see there was lots of history there, but still, Steve showed up, played well, and I think Dave was really happy.

But music was changing so much in the late 1980s. Dave was now an adult contemporary artist at a time when hair metal and grunge were taking over the world. It was getting harder and harder to break records like the one David just made, as good as it was. Very frustrating. We had a good time back then. I'll always believe that Dave is an undervalued talent. He's a monster guitar player and a phenomenal singer and songwriter. Sometimes I think that tends to get lost when rock 'n' roll history is written, but when you sit down and look at what he's done, there are very few like him.

Shouldn't Have Took More Than You Gave

Shouldn't have took more than you gave
Then we wouldn't be in this mess today
I know we've all got different ways
But the dues we've got to pay are still the same

It's time to change the script for this old play
You're reading and not feeling what you say
You're coming on too strong for me to stay
Interpret what you see in any way

It seems the simple things are hardest to explain
Winter's gonna come too soon and deaden all the pain
Footprints in the snow will show when things are still the same
Till you get the warmth of sun or someone to help you live again

Shouldn't have took more than you gave
Then we wouldn't be in this mess today
I know we've all got different ways
But the dues we've got to pay are still the same

Shouldn't have took more than you gave
Shouldn't have took more than you gave
Shouldn't have took more than you gave
Shouldn't have took more than you gave

CHAPTER EIGHTEEN

Shouldn't Have Took More Than You Gave

After recording *Two Hearts,* though I was happy with the album, there was nothing going on in the record world for me. Musical trends of the late 1980s had little space for classic singer/songwriters like me. On one hand, hair metal had exploded thanks to bands like Mötley Crüe, Quiet Riot, Poison, Def Leppard, and Guns N' Roses. On the other side of the coin were slick pop artists like Madonna, Paula Abdul, and Roxette, among others. It was also the era of MTV—and I was predominately known for my live shows.

The early '90s ushered in alternative rock subgenres, primarily grunge, which wiped out hair metal and a lot of hard rock. On top of that, electronic dance music, hip hop, and pop like Mariah Carey and Whitney Houston took over a large part of the commercial pie. I was all but invisible in the marketplace except for live concerts, and thank goodness I could make a living playing shows. I was on the road all the time.

I'd lived all over California, and nobody was knocking down my door, so I moved to Chicago. For one reason, it made more economic sense. Chicago was my favorite US city at that time. I loved the neighborhoods, the food, the museums. It's a major financial center. It's New York with a Midwest attitude. Plus, I had friends that could get things done, if you know what I mean. The local Italian social club had a picture of me and Frank Sinatra hanging on the wall. I think they really liked my music.

I still wasn't making the kind of money in music that I'd seen in the 1970s. I became open to offers outside the music industry, which is why I returned a call from a man named Jim Manera at the Leo Burnette Advertising Agency. This led me to some creative opportunities and, equally as important, a lifelong friendship with him. Making records, in my mind, was an exercise in futility, and perhaps I could develop musically in other ways. So I started developing commercial campaigns with Jim, mostly for beer clients.

Jim Manera was an advertising agent at Leo Burnett in Chicago who hired Dave for commercials. They remain close friends to this day.

Jim Manera:
In the 1980s I worked at big advertising agencies like the Leo Burnett company and DDB Worldwide, where I was responsible for a large portion of the Anheuser-Busch family of beers. Creatively, I always had a nice budget so I could basically work with almost any musicians I wanted to. At one point, I approached Dave Mason because I was a big fan of his, but he was locked into a Coors sponsorship, so he couldn't work with us. We wound up working with Neil Young, the Neville Brothers, The Allman Brothers Band, and Lynyrd Skynyrd, among other great artists. About a year after I first contacted Dave, my secretary buzzed me and said, "I have a Dave Mason on hold." I said to her, "Is he the new sales rep?" I never thought for a minute it could actually be the Dave Mason. When I got on the phone I said, "Is this really the Dave Mason?" He just laughed. Sure enough, it was him.

David was really into the advertising projects that I had going on in the late 1980s. I mean, he was open to anything. Music was changing, and I knew it was harder for him to command the audiences that he had a few years earlier. Everything was in flux in the business, and when we were marketing a new cold-

filtered beer for Anheuser-Busch, David came in with a very innovative track for
a commercial. He brought in terrific players like Mike Finnegan and other band
members of his to help make the commercial recording sessions truly unforgettable.
I remember one session he also brought an amazing harmonica player named
Sugar Blue who had made a name for himself years earlier playing on The Rolling
Stones' hit song "Miss You." He brought in some great female singers to do
the backgrounds, and along with all this talent, we recorded a really killer track.
Unfortunately, the client went with another concept, but this didn't take away from
the fact that I got to watch Dave Mason, up close and personal, play, sing, create,
and record. And, along the way of our working together, we became friends.

Though live music opportunities never slowed down, I experienced a
substantial decline in venue capacity and was no longer on top of multi-
artist billing. I had a relentless tour schedule, where it felt like I had to
work three times as hard for half the money. But it wasn't all a miserable
experience because Chicago, during that time, was an exciting place to
live. In spite of it all, I enjoyed myself a lot.

Pam and I had a beautiful apartment right on Lake Shore Drive
overlooking the lake and Grant Park. Our view of the Chicago Air Show
was unparalleled, and fireworks shows at the park looked like they were
coming through the window. I was out on the town all the time when
I wasn't touring, going to the great blues clubs, many of them open
until four in the morning: Kingston Mines, The Limelight (where I
took Patrick Swayze to go dancing), and Buddy Guy's. Cicero's, another
favorite, was open until six, closing only for a half hour to clean the bar.
And every act and entertainer who'd come to town would end up at
Faces. We'd love to go to Gibson's for great steaks and the best martinis
ever. Rosebuds on Taylor Street, Uno's for deep dish pizza, and there's
nothing like a Chicago hot dog or charred polish.

I got to play a concert on the floor of the Chicago stock exchange,
having been hired by my friend Chris Stewart. Another friend, Jim
McNulty, himself a fine folk singer and guitarist, became president of
the Chicago Mercantile. Paul and Sandy Antonello—music freaks who'd
attended several of my shows and who were also in the financial world—
became friends. I enjoyed an expanding social circle of people drawn
together by music but not in the business.

And, of course, there was Terry Cohen, one of my dearest and oldest
friends since coming to the US. We met back in the early 1970s when

he was comanaging the wonderful singer Minnie Ripperton. Hilarious and outrageous, Terry says things that most people think but don't have the guts to verbalize. This either leaves a crowd laughing hysterically or running away fast in the opposite direction. But Terry taught me a lot about loyalty; he'd do anything for someone he loved and very rarely do things for himself, if ever. I love him dearly. They broke the mold with Mr. Cohen, and it would take a whole other book to tell only half of the stories about my adventures by his side. Nick and Susan Pritzker became good friends and helped me more than once when things were on edge.

Chicago was good for a while, but then, like every other time, I needed to move on. Once a gypsy, always a gypsy. Not surprisingly, all this career shakeup, the harsh tour schedules, and ongoing financial woes took a toll on my marriage with Pam. Partly in an effort to save our relationship and partly because I wanted to escape—I don't know, *everything*—we moved to St. Thomas in the Virgin Islands.

Cool Runnin'

Do you look around and wonder if the world has passed you by
Everything keeps changing in the twinkling of an eye
You keep trying hard to just to turn it all around
Sometimes you got to let it slide, don't let it bring you down

And you gotta be cool, cool runnin'
Gotta be cool, cool runnin'
Gotta be cool, cool runnin'
From now on, from now on

No matter how much life may change, there's things that we still need
People keep on fighting over color, race, and creed
If you want to make this world a better place to be
You gotta look inside yourself, comes down to you and me

And you gotta be cool, cool runnin'
Gotta be cool, cool runnin'
Gotta be cool, cool runnin'
From now on, from now on

You gotta realize it's in your heart
It's those little lies that keep us all apart
You keep trying hard just to turn it all around
Sometimes you got to let it slide, don't let it bring you down

And you gotta be cool, cool runnin'
Gotta be cool, cool runnin'
Gotta be cool, cool runnin'
From now on, from now on

CHAPTER NINETEEN

Cool Runnin'

During the period when I'd been doing acoustic shows with Jim Krueger, I'd gotten an offer to do concerts in the US Virgin Islands—St. Croix and St. Thomas—in 1978 or so. I think sometime in my past I was a pirate because I instantly loved those islands. While on St. Croix I became friendly with a couple of West Indians, and, of course, I invited them to my show. I was told by the owners of the club that they couldn't come to my concert, guests or no guests. It was obvious there was severe racial discord on the island of St. Croix. St. Thomas was somewhat different and a little looser.

We found ourselves being booked at a place owned by Bill Grogan called Barnacle Bills, which was situated right in one of the harbors. A late-night club/bar with a large lobster on top of the roof, it was *the place* in the islands who'd hosted some singer/songwriter artists like Kenny Rankin and Jesse Colin Young. Our stage turned out to be some planks thrown across a lobster tank. It was here that I met who would become life-long friends: the Doumengs, Richard, Paul, David, and Laura. Their family owned the hotel we stayed at, Villa Olga, and Bolongo Bay, one of the first all-inclusive resorts, way before Sandals and the like.

In September 1989, I decided to move me and Pam to St. Thomas. Within two weeks of arriving, we were hit by Hurricane Hugo. That was one of the slowest moving storms ever—I think three miles an hour—and it lasted eight hours. We had a little yellow house up on the mountain overlooking the port of Charlotte Amalie. We spent most of the storm in

Boating around St. Thomas with Paul Doumeng and Richard Doumeng is still one of my favorite things to do.

the downstairs bathroom, which was at the back of the house up against the mountain. It seemed the most secure place. I filled the bathtub with water so that we would have some to drink in case the worst happened (which it did by the way), then I grabbed my favorite acoustic guitar and the cat, and Pam and I settled in waiting for nature to get down off its hind legs.

The storm sounded like several 747s taking off. After a few hours it subsided, but we were just going through the eye of the storm. Pretty soon, the winds picked up again, blowing in the opposite direction. You could feel the pressure; my ears clogged and head ached, and I decided to open up all the windows and doors on the main floor of the house and just let it all blow through. Not so crazy as it sounds. It's not the force of the wind that damages a house; it's more the barometric pressure that builds up, especially if everything is sealed. Whilst opening up the French doors of the living room, I stepped out on the balcony and screamed at the storm, not unlike the scene of Lieutenant Dan from *Forrest Gump* up in the crow's nest cursing the storm.

After the hurricane passed, there was water everywhere in the house, but all the windows, doors, and the roof were intact. Our biggest problem was a large tree that had come down across the driveway. We had no electricity, no running water, no food, and our best hope was to get down the mountain to Bolongo and the Doumengs. It took a couple of days to get the tree cleared so we could get out.

I can't say the rest of the island fared as well. It looked like an atomic bomb had been dropped. It was later that I learned that the hurricane was clocked at 200 mph sustained winds at the airport. Island locals, as well as tourists to the island, were all in the same straits with no electricity unless you had a generator or were staying at one of the hotels. Ice became more valuable than diamonds.

It's moments like this where you witness the best and the worst of people. While price gouging and all kinds of theft and greed was rampant, the Doumengs took us in, as they did a number of stranded people. Just to tell you what kind of people they are, they did it from a place of fairness and kindness. David Doumeng and I did the best we could to entertain guests stranded at their hotel and even got the local radio station to let us do a show,

The Dave & Dave Show, to help ease the tension on the island. You might ask yourself why I didn't just up and leave. It felt to me like a natural thing to stay and turn to entertaining. We would start the broadcast with "Ahh, the sounds of paradise," followed by the sound of drills and jackhammers. During all the reconstruction, we tried to keep a sense of humor for the islands—and, who am I kidding, for myself too. I'd never seen destruction

like that, not even in the war-torn England of my childhood.

I still visit St. Thomas and the Doumengs in Bolongo Bay as often as I can. While I didn't live there very long, it had a huge impact in terms of loving that place. But what I didn't know was that moving to an island paradise doesn't fix a marriage, and unfortunately, my marriage with Pam fell completely apart down there.

David Doumeng's family owned hotels in St. Thomas during the time Dave toured and lived there. Dave remains close friends with all the Doumeng family.

David Doumeng:

Dave Mason has definitely left his mark on St. Thomas. My family is from the Virgin Islands. We're a hotel family. We first met Dave at one of our hotels in about 1978. We had three of them. Dave came down there to play a gig at a small place, and he stayed at one of our properties. I was about nineteen years old. I was a singer/songwriter, gigging in local bars whenever I could. I wasn't as familiar with Dave's work as my older brother was. Judging from my brother's reaction to Dave's presence, I knew he was a big deal. He and I became friends right away. We really hit it off right from the beginning. He called me "Mowgli" after the character in The Jungle Book. *Dave was down there, playing acoustic shows with his partner Jim Krueger, and I was really blown away by what they did—just great songs. We would see him from time to time when he was doing acoustic shows. He moved to St. Thomas just before Hurricane Hugo struck in 1989.*

But then the hurricane hit. They were clocking 200 mile-per-hour sustained winds at the airport. Pretty much every place got devastated, and all the guests on the island were basically stranded. As locals, many of us got involved in helping to look after people and attend to those in need. Dave absolutely did his part. He came down from his house, which thankfully was not destroyed, to one of our places, the Lime Tree Hotel. He and I would put on shows each night for the guests to help them pass the time and forget all of the devastation around us. We even managed to write a song together called "Dig Me." People couldn't believe they were watching Dave Mason each night at a casual dinner. He really became a fixture after that, and we considered him to be part of our family and still do.

Soon after, Dave took me out on tour with him as an opening act all over the country, which was a huge deal for me. I'll never forget that. I got to play and expand my audience, and every night I got to watch Dave Mason onstage. I heard there were drugs going around, but I never really saw that much. I mean, all of us on the road were pretty much stoners, but I didn't see a lot of the cocaine that everybody talks about now.

Something unfortunate took place when Dave was on the road. I discovered that his wife was having an affair. There are no secrets on that island. How do I tell one of my best friends? When Dave came back from doing some shows, I sat him down and I told him straight out what was going on. He needed to know. First, he got understandably pissed off, but then he appreciated me having the guts to tell him the truth.

It was not long after that conversation that Dave left the island and moved back to the mainland. But we've always remained tight. He even sang at my wedding. No matter what happens, Dave Mason's legacy as one of the great guitar players of his generation will always be protected. I mean, timing is weird, and he came up in that era that featured so many great players from Clapton to Hendrix to Jeff Beck. But Dave totally holds his own.

I can't say I was shocked by the news about Pam. On one hand, I was overweight, I wasn't really taking care of myself at all, I was doing tons of cocaine, and I was basically a mess. But I was still out there constantly touring so that we could afford everything at home. I was working my ass off to make sure things were covered. And she goes off with a guy who lays cable for a living. It definitely stung. And hearing it the way that I heard it was also hard. You never want to be told that. It's a little bit humiliating and embarrassing.

I was still trying to figure out what the future held for me when I left the island. I felt confused, frustrated, and rudderless. Hurricane Hugo was sort of a metaphor for my life at that time.

But all great storms pass, and it's onward to the hard work of rebuilding.

Can't Stop Worrying, Can't Stop Lovin'

Who am I talking to; it's just myself
Talked to the wall when I talk to someone else
Only a few that I've met really knew
Why so many good things had so much abuse

I can't stop from worrying about the things we do
I can't stop from lovin'; without it nothin' would seem true

I've got my dreams about the way it's gonna be
I'd share it all with someone real, not make believe
It sometimes gets hard to see the wood from the tree
But when things are right, no questions will I need

I can't stop from worrying about the things we do
I can't stop from lovin'; without it nothin' would seem true

The scenery's changed but my feelings remain
Laughter and pain, and love are still the same
Something worth having doesn't come too easily
A man needs a challenge, or a man couldn't be
I can't stop from worrying about the things we do
I can't stop from lovin'; without it nothin' would seem true

CHAPTER TWENTY

Can't Stop Worrying, Can't Stop Lovin'

After my relationship with Pam came to its inevitable conclusion, I went back to Chicago to file for divorce, wondering if I'd be left penniless by the time it was all over. Chicago is called the can-do city, and Chicago sure did come through for me.

Terry Cohen came to me one day shortly after I'd come back, burst in the door without knocking, and declared, "Come on, we're getting divorced."

"What do you mean?" I asked.

"Just get in the car," he replied, and we drove out to a courthouse in one of the suburbs of Chicago.

There was nobody there. The courthouse was closed. "What's happening, Terry?" I asked, more than a little bewildered.

"The judge is going to meet us here. You're getting divorced. But you have to go in the courtroom yourself. I know this judge. I used to beat him up when we were kids at school."

I walked into the courthouse and into one of the courtrooms. It was just me and the judge. He looked at me and said, "Well, come on, let's get on with this. I have to get my kids to the dentist." He promptly stamped the papers and handed them to me. "You're divorced."

While my marital status changed, my nonstop touring did not. Then, six months after the official fall of the Berlin Wall, I got hired to tour

Russia, an out-of-the-blue invitation. It was going to be a goodwill tour and was put together by one of the members of the royal family of Japan along with a Russian promoter. The premise was that people with Harley Davidsons would pay a significant amount of money to tour the country, and we would be performing concerts along the way in various cities. It obviously sounded like a great adventure, and I thought it would be fun to take Terry on the trip.

We landed in St. Petersburg. The terminal at that time was like an enormous old airplane hangar. We were met by four limousines, which was how we would get around city to city. We took off into St. Petersburg, which, to me, was depressing. It looked like a beautiful room that had never been dusted. You could feel the lingering spirit of a socially repressed society. I almost started crying. The faces of the people reflected lifetimes that had been completely robbed of freedom. Russian rubles were worth nothing. Girls were selling themselves for a single American dollar. Wood chips were in toilet paper. And everything, I mean everything, was available to buy, including military hardware. It was the Eastern version of the Wild West and unlike anything I'd ever experienced.

Drummer Mark Ott snapped this image somewhere along the way. It's one of the only photos that survived the grueling Russian tour.

In every city we performed, we were hosted in government buildings for dinner parties—if you could even call them that. Long banquet tables were lined with bottles of Stolichnaya, with a full bottle in front of everybody. At least it was something to drink since the bottled water tasted like saltwater.

I forget what city we were in, but there was another event hosted in the Politburo, with a concert scheduled later that day. I went to the outdoor site to a stage similarly set up like what we'd have in the US. It had been raining all day, and the tarp over the stage was sagging, swollen heavy with rainwater. I climbed the stairs and saw that the entire platform was sheet metal. I said, "I'm sorry, but I will not perform on this stage," fearing the memory of one of my first band members—Michael Mann, who had been in The Jaguars with me back in the early 1960s—who had later been killed by electrocuting himself when he touched a mic on stage.

We had two busloads of KGB guys with us at all times, supposedly to protect us from the gypsies, which became necessary a couple of times. At night, we'd stop at different locations out in the middle of nowhere, surrounded only by dense forests. There would be barrels of gas for our cars, and people would be firing guns into the air for no apparent reason while the cars were refueled.

I was walking out of the hotel one day, about halfway through the tour, when Terry, who is one of the tougher guys I know, looked at me and said, "I'm leaving."

I looked at him for a minute and said, "If you leave me by myself, I'll never talk to you again." And I meant every word. Terry had just had enough of everything, just how shitty all the accommodations were and the supreme hassles, but thankfully he reconsidered and stayed on.

It was a concept and a tour that had great intentions, but experientially it was the longest ten days of my life. Before we left, my drummer, Mark Ott, had been beaten in an elevator in one of the hotels. My keyboard player was a nervous wreck, in such a state that we had to find a doctor, which we finally did. When we went to his office, we were greeted by this rather tall gentleman in a white lab coat, not unlike Uriah Heep—very thin with a hook nose, and I'll never forget his long, spiderlike fingers. He wore a patch over one eye, and there was one bare lightbulb in the room. It was time for me to go home.

There were some more dates to be done, but I explained to our tour representative that I just couldn't finish it. I offered to return the money, but he was gracious enough to say, "That's fine, don't worry about it." I arranged to get the band out and told Terry to find us any first-class flight out of there, whether it was headed toward Chicago or not. The first available was Vienna. We booked it and got the hell out of Russia.

Once safely in Vienna, we found a nice hotel. Terry found us the best restaurant in the city for dinner. The next day we headed to sweet home Chicago.

We made it home but never saw any of our musical equipment from the Russian tour again.

Mark Ott was a drummer with the Dave Mason Band during the late '80s and early '90s and was on Dave's tour of Russia.

Mark Ott:
Russia with Dave Mason is something I'll never forget. Originally, I got called to do a drumming session with Dave. He needed a drummer that had a different kind of feel, and I was recommended. I did the session, then a couple of years later, Dave's office called me for an audition, and then Dave asked me if I had proper cases for my drums. I was so excited. I figured that meant that I had gotten the gig. I got home and my fax machine started blowing up, sheets and sheets of paper with tons of gigs on it. Before we hit the road, we did what Dave called a "throwaway gig" at a place called Buddy Mulligan's in Chicago. We did a sound check at about five in the afternoon, and then I actually went home because it was near where I lived. When I got back that night, the place was absolutely packed and there were lines around the block. That's when I started getting a sense about how intense Dave Mason fans were. I think we did about twenty-six dates in thirty-one days around the country. It was crazy.

Throughout 1990–91 we toured with Edgar Winter, Poco, and lots of other people. Dave became like a mentor to me. He taught me how to not be nervous, how to be confident and calm when I went out on stage. That was really his thing. He was the coolest cat you'd ever see play. Nothing phased him. When it was showtime, he just went out there and killed it. Confident as could be.

And then came the invitation to go to Russia. The vibe over there in general was pretty exciting. People were smelling freedom. The wall had just come down, and the world was really changing over there. It was amazing to be thrown into the middle of it. But there was something shady about the whole thing. The promoters were supposedly tied up with the Russian mafia, and we were guarded at all times by these ex-KGB agents who really had our backs. I remember they all reminded me of Ivan Drago from Rocky IV. Whenever these guys sensed trouble, they would step in and protect us. Everything started off in St. Petersburg Square, and there were thousands of people there. I think we played a great show, but from there things got a little bit weird. Some of the shows were just thrown together at the last minute.

We flew home to JFK in New York City. Incredibly, none of our gear made it back. We were set to play a gig at Poplar Creek about a week later, and Dave was going to cancel it because we had no equipment. But bassist Wally Hustin and I went crazy. That was our childhood place where we saw so many famous shows, and we were dying to play there. Dave said, "Listen, if you can get the gear together, we'll do it." And so we did. What a memorable gig that was on July 26, 1992. We played there along with Richie Havens, Robby Krieger, Roger McGuinn, and The Band.

I'll always value the time I spent playing with Dave Mason. The catchphrase "I love you, man" from the beer commercials was really big at the time, and I always said that to Dave on the road. Because I meant it. I learned so much from him. Each night I knew I was in the presence of something and someone really special. With Dave, I realized that every note has a meaning. Every single note he played belonged, and nothing was ever wasted or thrown away.

Blow by Blow

It's always something, or it ain't nothing at all
It's feast or famine, too hot or out in the cold
So here we stand, alone together, our backs against the wall
If my heart wasn't in it, I wouldn't be here at all

Blow by blow, well it's blow by blow
Here we go again, well it's blow by blow

Coming off the ropes and fighting for the hope in us all
Are you in my corner, or playing both sides of the wall
So make a stand, It's now or never, 'cause life is much too short
And if your heart isn't in it, you shouldn't be here at all

Blow by blow, well it's blow by blow
Yet here we go again, and it's blow by blow
Blow by blow, well it's blow by blow
I'm back on my feet again, well it's blow by blow

I can almost see through the tears and I've got my pride
The dreams that I've hidden for years just won't be denied

So here we stand, alone together, our backs against the wall
If my heart wasn't in it, I wouldn't be here at all

Blow by blow, well it's blow by blow
Here we go again, and it's blow by blow
Blow by blow, well it's blow by blow
I'm back on my feet again, and it's blow by blow

CHAPTER TWENTY-ONE

Blow by Blow

On March 29, 1993, I lost Jim Krueger. He was living with his brother Rich in Manitowoc, Wisconsin, where he was from. On that day in March, he succumbed to complications related to years of alcohol abuse—chiefly, pancreatitis. He was only forty-three years old. I made plans to go to his funeral, but the weather was incredibly bad that day, and the drive from Chicago became impossible.

I still think about Jim a lot, especially when I sing his song, "We Just Disagree." He had such a wonderful disposition about him and was just an outstanding guitar player. Check him out on the *Certified Live* album and his playing on "Going Down Slow," and you'll see precisely what I mean. I was fortunate to have him as a musical partner for as long as I did. He always had my back, onstage and otherwise. I have no doubt we would still be making music together if he was still around.

I eventually made my way back to California. Things were at a major lull career wise for no other reason than I had exhausted all my opportunities in Chicago and every place I had lived. California, being the first real place I landed in the States, always felt like a safe haven for me. It was only natural for me to return.

Further thoughts from Dave's friend Jim Manera, who hired him to do commercial work in Chicago.

Jim Manera:
Around 1989, I moved to Los Angeles. Dave and (then wife) Pam moved to St. Thomas and had a wonderful life down in the islands for a while. Or so I thought. A couple of years later, Dave showed up on my doorstep with a suitcase. "Do you have room for me?" He and his wife had split, and he had nowhere else to go. So he moved in with me for a little while.

A few weeks later I said, "We need a coming out party for you." So we went up to the Trancas bar in Malibu. Robin Trower was playing, and the room was packed. We were watching the show, and on my right, was a tall, lanky guy who turned out to be Mick Fleetwood. He and Dave got reacquainted that night, and soon Dave was in Fleetwood Mac. He always bounces back.

Dave is still one of my best friends. I think of him like a big brother, a shoulder where I can always share things that nobody else knows. I also think David is the best kept secret in rock 'n' roll. When you listen closely to what he does, you realize he's in a league by himself.

I have found over the years that some of the most significant things come out of the blue when you least expect them. I was pleasantly surprised one afternoon when I answered the phone and it was Mick Fleetwood.

"Dave, I'm thinking of putting together a reformed version of Fleetwood Mac," he said. "Would you be interested?"

Due to the way things were at that particular time, "interested" was an understatement. "Yes," I said immediately. "Of course I would be interested. Let's get together and talk."

Stevie Nicks and Lindsey Buckingham had long since left Fleetwood Mac, and there wasn't much going on with the band. There was to be an album with a new lineup, which was me, Mick, John McVie, Christine McVie, Billy Burnette, and Bekka Bramlett, daughter of Delaney and Bonnie Bramlett, whom I'd held in my arms years earlier when she was just a baby. It had all the ingredients for making a really good record. I assumed we'd be recording each of the songs as a band. We'd learn the songs together until we had them down, and then we'd record them all at the same time in order to capture some of that energy that happens when you play live. You know, how a band typically works. I was more than a little surprised when Mick said, "We've never recorded like that."

Since the tracks were being cut with me playing with Mick, or Mick playing with Christine, or some other combination, there were never more than two or three people at one time recording. On top of that, Christine McVie didn't want me playing on any of her songs, and she also said she wouldn't be out on the road with us to promote it. During the making of the album, we did a lot of touring in the US and Europe. I got to play some places I'd never been, one of which is still one of my favorite cities, Venice, Italy.

Our album, *Time,* was released in 1995. It is one of the least known of any Fleetwood Mac albums, but I had two songs on it, "Blow by Blow" and "I Wonder Why." There were plans for us to tour the following year to promote it, but things were about to abruptly change, almost as quickly as the opportunity had appeared. Bekka, Billy, and I were informed that Stevie and Lindsey were rejoining the band. *Time* was not *Rumours,* but it was a good album. Once Warner Bros. knew that Nicks and Buckingham were coming back to the group, however, they dropped all promotion on *Time.*

This news came shortly after I'd just read in *Billboard* magazine that Traffic, with Winwood and Capaldi, were going to tour. But I wasn't included. In fact, Winwood said my role in Traffic was no more than "an invited guest," to which Mick Fleetwood said, "Well, we have been very happy to have you with us as an invited guest!" I could not believe how

Winwood had dismissed my efforts. I'd written hits for the band. I'd been a founding member in every sense of the term.

Musically, my time in Fleetwood Mac didn't feel like being in a band since the entire creative process was so disjointed. Financially, however, this was a helpful chapter for me. Even though things ended on a bittersweet note, Mick and I still maintain a really good friendship to this day. In fact, we still play together. If you're visiting Hawaii, you just might catch us playing somewhere on Maui.

Mick Fleetwood is the acclaimed drummer, cofounder, and leader of the legendary band Fleetwood Mac. Dave and Mick are close friends.

Mick Fleetwood:
David really is part of a rare breed that definitely goes back to Traffic. I was slightly in awe of them. Theirs was such a strange art form. Sometimes as a musician, sociologically speaking, you look back at things, and you realize there was really something deeper happening at that time. It was that way with The Beatles. But it really was hard for me to wrap my head around Traffic. Why is that? I don't really understand it. There's a saxophone player, what is that? It was so groundbreaking in so many ways. An eclectic bunch of people at odds with each other, which was always part of their story. They were so bright you almost knew they were going to burn out, almost like Cream. But it was so bright that we still talk about it today. I didn't know David back then. But I knew of him. I remember seeing him at a place called the Speakeasy in London and thinking to myself, "Oh, my God, that's Dave Mason." Like, that was the reverence that we held him in. He was part of this entity called Traffic, which automatically made him special. And he was dressed so beautifully and stylishly. But we didn't know each other back then. As time went on, of course, he went his own way, released Alone Together, *and he became this beautiful*

solo artist. We opened for him, which was always a thrill, but then he wound up opening up for us!

Our truly personal music history happened in the early 1990s when I asked him to join Fleetwood Mac. It was a strange timeframe. But I genuinely thought he was the right piece at the right time. He was a known entity; it was a huge load to take on, but he certainly didn't need to prove himself. He was Dave Mason, after all. When I asked him if he wanted to give it a try, he was quite interested, and off we went. I recently heard some tapes from that time period, and it was a wonderful band. Honestly? Listening to it today, that band had the wrong name. It should've been called The Dave Mason Band because he really helped us take things to the next level. There were some great moments, but it didn't go all the way that we wanted. It was probably a bridge too far, but we gave it our best. That version of Fleetwood Mac was obviously very important because it got us to the next level when Stevie and Lindsey came back.

But we didn't do it simply to create a bridge to the next version. We did it because, at that moment, it felt like the right thing to do. My band has always had these moments of survival where you bring in new blood to get to the next level. That's part of Fleetwood Mac's history, and Dave is certainly an important part of that. I love the recipe myself, but back then Dave would say to me, "This is all too much drama." I would tell him that's how I survived all of these years, with the drama, and he would just laugh and say he never could survive with the sorts of things that we went through. That's just Dave.

When I think of Dave, I think an important part of his legacy is how he can own something that's not even his property. How he can take pivotal songs like "All Along the Watchtower" and bring a magic to it because he's so connected to it. He can do things with it that make it his own. I've been so spoiled over the years when it comes to guitar players, from Peter Green to Lindsey Buckingham to Danny Kerwin to Bob Welsh to Jeremy Spencer. I think I know good guitar players. And when I sit and listen to Dave Mason, I know I'm listening to someone with a very powerful ability to make things his own. Recently, I was sitting with him at his home, and he was playing me some new music. I just sat back and said quietly, "You are one hell of a guitar player." He looked to me and said, "Really? You really think so?" And we both started laughing. "Yes," I told him, "you're a fucking great guitar player."

The 1990s also had a false start with Ringo Starr playing in his All-Starr touring band, which included Peter Frampton, Gary Booker, Jack Bruce, Simon Kirke, and me. We were well into rehearsals, which had been a bit difficult for me. Since I don't read or write music, I'd been asking for "cheat" sheets, which I never received, so I was just feeling my way through things. There were a few other little issues that were brewing throughout the rehearsal process—not unexpected, of course, when you get a group of artists together. Originally, we were all informed that we would be traveling on Ringo's private plane throughout the tour. And then, little by little, that started to get revised. We band members would be demoted to riding around on buses most of the time while he flew on the plane. Nobody in the band seemed too happy about that.

This was also my "midlife crisis" period where I had taken up with a very beautiful, very young stripper who looked exactly like Marilyn Monroe. She was a Southern belle whom I had met through Seka, the well-known adult film actress (aka Dorothea Patton). I had gotten to know Seka through Terry back in Chicago. Anyway, the basic rule during rehearsals and so on was that you were not to bring girlfriends or wives around. The only woman that was allowed was Barbara Bach, who was with Ringo. So, my stripper friend created all kinds of commotion that didn't exactly endear me to everyone.

At the outset of rehearsals, I'd informed the powers that be that on the last day of rehearsal I would have to leave early to catch a redeye flight to Philadelphia to play a prescheduled solo show, then jet back for the start of the Ringo tour. Well, evidently things had not been communicated correctly to Mr. Starr.

Ringo: "Where are you going, Dave?"

Me: "To catch a plane for a show."

Ringo: "Well, cancel it."

Me: "No. I have a show. I informed everyone early on."

Ringo: "Cancel it!"

Me: "Buy me a new ticket or pay me to cancel the show!"

And off I went. En route back east, I started getting a barrage of calls from various attorneys of all stripes begging me, "Dave, please call Ringo and sort this out. He's a Beatle!" A call was set up for me to talk to Ringo. It started out pleasantly enough. I explained to him again that I had a prior contractual agreement, and I'd given everybody in his organization enough notice about this. Then, he got more and more pissed off and started yelling at me on the phone. So I hung up.

That was my last communication with Mr. Starkey (along with the end of my tenure in the All-Starr Band). I'm disappointed it ended that way. I would have loved to share the stage with those artists. But life is where it's at—and we have to meet it there.

L-R: Mark Rivera, Jack Bruce, Dave, Ringo, Simon Kirke, Peter Frampton, Gary Brooker

Full Circle and Then

Seems such a long, long time
Since I let somebody into this heart of mine
I've come from a long, long way
Took a roller coaster ride to find an empty place
Now's the time to let it be
Take those broken hearts entwined, just set them free

And come full circle 'cause now I see

Nothing matters, only you and me
Let's come full circle and make amends
Start it over and be the best of friends
Let's come full circle, and then

Drifted from day to day
I had it all but let it slip away
I ain't the kind to gamble small
I bet my heart and, baby, lost it all
Can I take this soul of mine
Can these broken hearts entwined ever mend

And come full circle 'cause now I see
Nothing matters, only you and me
Let's come full circle and make amends
Start it over and be the best of friends
Let's come full circle, and then

CHAPTER TWENTY-TWO

Full Circle and Then

I was back in California doing solo tours and looking for somewhere to rent that was close enough to LA but far enough away to not to pay LA prices. Leigh Taylor Young and I were seeing each other once again, though not living together. She mentioned Ojai, which I'd not been to since 1969.

It was there that I found the perfect place. Only three houses overlooked Lake Casitas, one of which I rented. My objective was to create a similar situation to the Traffic cottage, somewhere somewhat isolated, in nature, and with a lot of room.

I essentially turned the whole house into a recording studio. Every room except the kitchen had recording equipment. One of the upstairs bedrooms was converted into a control room, and my bedroom had a set of drums in front of the fireplace.

During that period, I'd reconnected with Jim Capaldi for what became The 40,000 Headmen Tour. The shows were fairly successful, and a live album came out of it. The most notable part of the tour was doing shows at the Bottom Line in New York City. George Harrison came to the show on the first night, and I wished I'd asked him to sit in. Jim told me Steve Winwood was in town and was probably going to come watch one of the shows. "Great," I said, and I meant it.

Winwood came on the second night, and Capaldi was in a dither. So was the audience. They knew Winwood was there, meaning three of the four original Traffic members were in the same room together. I couldn't miss the opportunity, so I introduced him from the stage and called out, "Why don't you come up and do something with us?" Jim had his back to the audience when I said it and proceeded to shoot me a look.

"What the fuck are you doing, man?" Jim hissed at me. The audience was going a little crazy, so there wasn't much Winwood could do but get on stage. I can't remember exactly, but I think we did a version of "Low Spark," "High Heeled Boys," and then "Gimme Some Lovin'." The audience went ape shit as we left the stage and went together into the small dressing room backstage.

It was obvious we were going to have to come back out for another song. I looked at Steve and suggested we do "Dear Mr. Fantasy." I proposed that Winwood would play organ, I'd play guitar, and Capaldi would play drums. Steve shook his head no and said, "I *have* to play guitar." That would have been fine and well if we had a second rig. But since we only had one, and I don't play keyboards, it didn't make musical sense.

"You can have the last song," I pleaded, "just play keys and sing. Come on! They want to see all three of us." I was practically begging.

"No," he shot back emphatically. "I *have* to play guitar."

I asked several times, but he still refused. His then-wife looked at Steve and said, "This isn't going to work. Mason is nothing but a redneck."

And that was that. So Capaldi and I went back up for the encore, sadly without Winwood, and did "We Just Disagree." From the audience's reaction, it didn't seem to matter that Winwood didn't join us.

Me and Jim and catching up with George Harrison backstage during the tour.

I went back to my home in Lake Casitas, and I started working on what I still consider one of my better albums, *26 Letters and 12 Notes*. Creating in the peace and space of the country was like going back to the cottage days with Traffic, which is, as I said, exactly what I had intended with the place. When I was finished, I felt sure there was a label that would pick it up.

The first person I took it to was Ahmet Ertegun. Ahmet loved the album. But I'd been out of the business for some time and wasn't really prepared for the fact we were in the era of consensus—meaning even though Ahmet was chairman of the board of Warner Communications, even he didn't have the power to push an album to market. Dave Mason, apparently, was no longer a going concern. No other major label was interested.

Jim Capaldi was staying with me and participated in songwriting, and we did some recording together. I still had solo dates to do, and unfortunately when I came back off a short run, I found Capaldi was gone, and some tapes were missing from my studio. That was the last time I saw Jim Capaldi—until 2004, that is, when we were inducted into the Rock & Roll Hall of Fame.

Just a Song

Don't talk to me of fame or fortune
Don't tell me of the things you've read
Don't get involved in games of reason
There ain't no reason I could see for you to win

I've asked you questions now for far too long
I'm feelin' highly wasted, but there ain't no sun
I'm tired of callin' you here when things go wrong
So now I'm finding all I need in just a song

Just take my hand and let me feel that I belong
Just take some time out from yourself to get along
Just one more day and I will turn from you and run
Although you're all I do, all I've ever done

I've asked you questions now for far too long
I'm feelin' highly wasted but there ain't no sun
I'm tired of callin' you here when things go wrong
So now I'm finding all I need in just a song

It may be the way I feel but you are all I have
It's not the same for everyone I know that well
It needs a lot of give and take from everyone
But playin' games just won't help us get along

I've asked you questions now for far too long
I'm feelin' highly wasted, but there ain't no sun
I'm tired of callin' you here when things go wrong
So now I'm finding all I need in just a song

It's just a song, just a song

CHAPTER TWENTY-THREE

Just a Song

Early one morning in 2003, I received a phone call. "Congratulations, Dave," the voice on the other end greeted me. It was someone representing the Rock & Roll Hall of Fame. "You're being inducted as a founding member of Traffic." I was told we were being inducted along with Prince, ZZ Top, Jackson Browne, The Dells, Jann Wenner, and Bob Seger. Honestly, I'm lukewarm on awards in general, but this was really meaningful. I had such musical highs and lows since those Traffic days, sideswiped hazards of the business, and fought off innumerable personal demons. I was finally focused back on the music by that point. And then this call. I was honored and thrilled. I was being acknowledged as more than just an invited guest.

But I was also curious. How was this all going to play out, given the strain—both historic and in real time—with Winwood and, to some extent, Capaldi? I never did hear another word about those tapes that Jim seemed to have run off with, and I didn't feel like opening that can of worms.

Nothing was ever easy with Traffic—not even this wonderful recognition. Rather than any kind of discussion between me, Winwood, and Capaldi about what song we would perform, I got an e-mail from Winwood's management saying that we were going to perform "Dear Mr. Fantasy" as it was originally recorded. I played bass on the record, but I hadn't played bass in over forty years. I didn't even own one. And copying the record was never what Traffic was about. We were originally a jam band. We were progressive and never played our concerts to sound exactly like our records. The idea of presenting Traffic that way was odd to me. I mean, Dave Matthews was chosen to induct us. If that didn't crystallize our cred as one of the first real "jam" bands, then what did? And why couldn't we properly honor that legacy?

So, I wrote back and suggested that instead we plan a standout performance for the night of the induction ceremony. That we stretch it out and make it something special by trading guitar licks, rather than just replicating the record. Wasn't the point of the Rock & Roll Hall of Fame not only to show up for the music we'd created but also to highlight the artists we'd become? I received an e-mail back saying, "That's not going to happen."

I wasn't going to play bass. The instrument requires a certain feel, and I didn't have a feel for it, having lost interest in playing bass some three decades back. Jamming on guitars was not even open for discussion, so I wrote back to say I'd play acoustic guitar for the sake of being out there together with the band. I thought it was a nonintrusive way of participating. I suggested that Will Lee, who is one of the best bass players in the country, could sit in to cover that part since I wasn't going to do it.

I got a third e-mail, again saying, "That's not going to happen."

Since his management was dictating the terms with no input from the rest of us, it was clear this was turning into a Steve Winwood performance, not a Traffic performance. I decided I'd rather just sit it out.

I received a phone call from Ahmet, asking me to please reconsider. I explained everything to him, and while he was disappointed and didn't agree with my decision, he understood. Two days later I got a call from Paul Shaffer, who would be the band leader for the ceremony. "Hey, Dave," he said. "Don't shoot the messenger, but I've been told to ask you about the performance." I again explained myself. "Well," he said, "at the end of the Rock & Hall of Fame show, all the artists get up and jam on one song. We all decided we want to do "Feelin' Alright?" Well now. This was a great compliment from fellow musicians whom I respected a lot. It sort of softened the sting that I would not be performing with Traffic. But I've always thought the music was bigger than the band, and in spite of it all, my story of music is one that transcends the greatest of obstacles.

As it turned out, not only would I not be performing with Traffic, I wasn't even invited to sit with Jim and Steve at the table set aside for the band. They, along with their guests, were settled in with engineer Eddie Kramer several tables away from me. I had brought some friends with me, and from our table down the way, I made eye contact at one point with Jim, but that was about it. Prince, who was also being inducted, opened the show with a dazzling version of his song "Let's Go Crazy." He also did "Sign o' the Times" and "Kiss." I had never seen him perform live before, and I was blown away. In fact, the thought in my head was, "Thank God I'm not playing up there with Traffic tonight because they have to follow this." Prince is the last guy you want to go on after. That was proven again later in the evening when he came out and jammed on the George Harrison song "While My Guitar Gently Weeps" along with Tom Petty and others.

Eventually we went up to accept our award, but none of us looked at each other. We just made our speeches and stepped aside.

Then it came time for the all-star jam at the end. It was funny seeing Steve Winwood over the keyboards before "Feelin' Alright?" started. Sadly, he didn't seem too happy about that. Yet, all in all, it was a great experience sensing all of those legends on either side of me as I stepped up to the microphone to sing the first verse of the song that I had given Traffic so many years earlier. Feeling Keith Richards, Tom Petty, ZZ Top, and Jackson Browne all play on my song really did become the ultimate kind of vindication for me. Jim was on the congas, but we didn't really look at each other. I was just focused on being steady and playing a good guitar solo. To be honest, it was kind of a blur. But I remember feeling happy inside that the ending worked out the way that it did.

After the jam was over, I heard a lot of nice comments from everybody on the stage. Moments later, I found myself in the elevator with Steve and Jim going back up to our rooms at the Waldorf. There wasn't a word between us at all, just silence as the elevator delivered us upstairs to our separate rooms.

And that's how the evening ended. It was a night I'll always remember, though bittersweet. It was a missed opportunity for Traffic to come together and make some new magic.

Give Me a Reason Why

Give me a reason for giving, give me a reason to take
Give me a reason for loving, Daddy, won't you give me a reason to hate
Give me a reason for laughter, give me a reason to cry
Give me a reason for living, Daddy, won't you give me a reason why
Won't you give me a reason why

Looking at me with those big blue eyes, asking me things that I just can't describe
Daddy, who's God, and what's on his mind? That's a good question, I reply
Tell me a story, or sing me a song; don't make it too short, don't make it too long
Tell me the difference between right and wrong, in time all these answers will come
   along
In time all these answers will come along

Fly like a silver bird, cry on a broken word, follow your dreams
Laying foundations for new generations; think of the good things you'll see

Fly like a silver bird, cry on a broken word, follow your dreams
Laying foundations for new generations, think of the good things you'll see
Give me a reason for giving, give me a reason to take
Give me a reason for loving, Daddy, Won't you give me a reason to hate
Give me a reason for laughter, Give me a reason to cry
Give me a reason for living, Daddy, won't you give me a reason why
Won't you give me a reason why?

CHAPTER TWENTY-FOUR

Give Me a Reason Why

I received a phone call early one morning in 2006. My son True, thirty-five years old, was dead, found alone, all by himself on the floor of his Florida apartment. Suicide or overdose; we'd never know. Either way, it cut me to the bone.

To put one step in front of the other each day since that call has, frankly, been more difficult than I, a songwriter by nature, can put into words. That alone may sound like a cliché, something trite and pedestrian, but the death of a child robs you of a certain part of your imagination. I'm not sure how you can shake pain like that; I'm positive no parent does. And I'm not sure we are meant to. I believe some things happen to you that don't ever disappear but just dissolve into the character you become; the backbone of your being.

They say one of the hardest things to do is outlive your children, and I know that's true. My son's death felt all the more distressing because I had to reconcile the fact, yet again, that I'd been devoted to my career. My eyes were not and had not been on my home life. I had never been a traditional father and never would. I don't say that to sound callous. I say that because to suggest otherwise would be the antithesis of my late son's name.

Even then, one has to wonder. Would True have lived had I taken him on tour more as a child and beyond? If I had been more present? I'm not so sure; and only a fool intent on punishing themselves would ponder these questions. It would drive even the sanest person mad. All I know is that I wish I could reach out to him—then, and now. He will always be my own "Tears in Heaven."

With time, though, death has a way of helping you make more meaning out of life. Because my life on the road has been substantial, the vast majority of my days find me away from home. My touring band and crew are like family; my fans are, too. They are what makes the tour wheel turn.

Namaste

Namaste, namaste, namaste, namaste, namaste
Why worry, ain't nothing gonna last forever
Why worry about the winds of change
Why worry, everybody's gonna get what they've got comin'
Why worry, let yourself be saved

One love
Getting down with aloha feeling, one love
Namaste, namaste, namaste, one love
Bringing in the aloha feeling, one love

Tune in, open up and let love begin
Why worry, take it to your heart
Why worry, can we all ever get together
Who knows, who dares, who's got the will to really care

One love
Getting down with aloha feeling, one love
Namaste, namaste, namaste, one love
Bringing in the aloha feeling, one love

CHAPTER TWENTY FIVE

Namaste

In 2005, I was still playing a number of shows, going and going, as I know how to do. I'd also started cleaning up my cocaine act. I was getting too old for that shit. I'd been hired to play a private birthday party in Reno for twins, these guys named Gene and Glenn Carano. It would be at the Eldorado, one of their many casinos.

I don't remember what song I was on when a firecracker caught my eye. You know that feeling? I hope you do. I hope we all have that one moment of recognition.

She was one of those elegantly long-boned women who are tiny at the same time. She was wearing sleek black leather pants, had waist-length blonde hair, and heels that would topple her over if she drank another sip of the white wine in her glass. She appeared as curious and fascinated by the world as Alice in the looking glass.

I was riveted. Her giant blue eyes traveled over my face, and I traveled to another time. I smiled like I hadn't smiled in years.

I asked my assistant to go into the audience to find out who she was. Her name?

Winifred.

And, ahem, she was married.

Still, we all (including her husband) gathered together afterward to drink, chat, and get to know each other. I had a feeling it would not be the last time I saw her.

Winifred and I kept in communication over the next few years. Whenever I was playing in Tahoe, Winifred and her husband would come to the show and say hello backstage. One year when I was playing Harrah's in Tahoe, though, I found out that Winifred was in the midst of a separation. She came to Tahoe to take me to lunch, and lunch turned into breakfast. She had no idea who I was when we first met; she had no sense of my music or what I had done or been through. Evidently, it was my scintillating personality that won her over.

We both, admittedly, had issues. She was entangled with alcohol, and I was unwinding from my affinity for cocaine. Though we had a ton of fun together, ours wasn't the making of a stable relationship.

Still, Winifred started spending more time with me in Ojai, where I'd moved from Lake Casitas and had just purchased a house, my first home since Mariposa. I'd been in the area, in Lake Casitas, but my new place was in the east end, with a 180-degree view of the entire valley. Ojai, California, is nestled in a magnificently beautiful valley—the only one in the state that runs east and west, so the sun shines most of the day. For me (and many others) it is one of the most peaceful places on the planet. And, since Ojai is one of the last remaining places still filled with orange groves, the scent of orange blossoms fills the valley twice a year. It's magical and bucolic. In some ways it reminds me of Worcester, England.

A few months after she began staying with me, Winifred said, "I'm going to get sober." She placed herself at the Recovery Ranch in Tennessee where, indeed, she quit drinking and embarked on the work of rebuilding her life. She never asked for any financial help, or anything else for that matter. She is headstrong and disciplined like that. When she gets something in her head, she's like a dog on a bone. At the end of her program, we spoke. I let Winifred know that I supported her sobriety but was still going to enjoy a glass of wine or two from time to time.

"Are you OK with that?" I asked tentatively.

"Yes," she said—and firmly at that. "Sobriety is my path and not necessarily for everybody else."

I was in the process of remodeling the house and, luckily for Winifred, I'd doubled the size of my closet. It was during this time that she moved in permanently and came with a full wardrobe and more shoes than anyone I'd ever seen in my life. She had come from a successful career in the art world, with seven locations in three states, including Lahaina, Las Vegas, and San Francisco, as well as some property in downtown Reno. But between getting sober and her divorce, she'd lost almost everything.

Even in that state, her generosity shined almost as much as her open, glittering smile. She offered to help pay for some of the remodeling projects, which I refused.

Winifred and I are polar opposites in many ways, but as Mr. Spock from *Star Trek* said, "Differences combine to form meaning and beauty." That is certainly true in our case. Being with Winifred is one of the best decisions I've ever made in my life; she is my most valuable asset, a remarkably creative, caring, and patient woman.

My love for her doesn't mean thunderstorms don't still brew in the house from time to time. We hit a speed bump at one point that took some working through. Though Winifred started teaching yoga before she left Reno, she threw herself into it in earnest in Ojai after she completed recovery. She practiced every day in a studio downtown where she also started teaching again. I was on the road touring practically nonstop. When I came home, I would find things that I would never consider buying: Buddha sculptures, chandeliers, flowers. Roses and vases, and a tiny picture of George Harrison she kept next to her computer as her muse. Necklaces from dead yogic gods. It was all so damn *feminine*. My home felt alien to me, and I have to admit I was getting resentful because whenever I'd be off the road, Winifred was gone. She'd be in town, doing something at that yoga studio she loved so much. We were technically living in the same place but in two different worlds.

Those tensions could have broken us up. Instead, I invited Winifred into the family business.

At first, she wasn't thrilled. Give up her life as a yoga teacher to live *on the road?*

One of her many outstanding attributes, though, is that, when push comes to shove, she's down to earth and practical. She agreed to come on the next tour.

This is a girl from Highland Park in Dallas, Texas. She wasn't brought up to ramble around with some musician, but I wanted more time together more than anything. This was a huge reach for her, but damn if she didn't throw herself into it. In the middle of the chaos of the road, she'd always find somewhere to do her yoga. She still does to this day. It's interesting to watch someone practice yoga in the narrow hallway of a

Prevost bus going seventy miles per hour on an open stretch of highway. But that's her. She is anything but square.

Our lives began to blend, though aforementioned storms would roll through the tour bus occasionally. She documented her journey in a beautifully written book called *Downdog for Roaddogs,* and I encourage anyone to read it. It's poignant, funny, and a wonderful invitation for anyone looking to start the practice of yoga.

Since there was little chance of any Traffic reunion coming together, I came up with a tour concept called Traffic Jam. We'd feature not only my songs, but also a number of Traffic songs, many of which I hadn't played in years. Since it was after the financial collapse of 2008, I was concerned about what kind of audiences there would be, afraid, I'll admit, it would be just performing to tables and chairs.

To my pleasant surprise, it was one of the more successful tours in recent years. The phone started ringing again, and I started getting bigger audiences and better venues. Touring began to take on new life. And when I was off the road, which is a rarity, I was back in my studio making music again. In 2014, I put out a CD called *Future's Past* (Graham Nash's 1976 painting of me is the cover), and in 2015, I put out a live CD of the Traffic Jam tour. The releases kept coming. In 2017 I released *Pink Lipstick* and in 2018 a live CD called *4Real Rock & Soul Revue* from my tour with rock legend Steve Cropper. I was just about to release *Alone Together Again* in 2020 when we got shut down in the pandemic. Since then, it has been released.

I'd wanted to make a blues album forever, and in between and among all the touring I finally have. *A Shade of Blues*, though not a blues album in the strictest sense (with the exception of "Dust My Blues"), was a fulfilling endeavor. The highlight for me was playing and recording with Joe Bonamassa and Steve Cropper during a spontaneous session while in Nashville. Some of my best work and favorite musical moments happen like that. Touring in 2018 with Steve Cropper was a thrill. The influence of Booker T. and the M.G.'s, for me, cannot be overstated. You have to step back to the early days and look at the roots of rock and roll. What is commonly referred to as the British Invasion is really an American story. It goes back to the days of Glenn Miller, Tommy Dorsey, and Duke Ellington; the great masters of the organ, Jimmy Smith, Jack McDuff, Jimmy McGriff; the great blues influences such as Freddie King, Albert King, B. B. King, Elmore James, Bobby Parker, Buddy Guy, Otis Rush, Ray Charles; and the early influences of Elvis Presley, Eddie Cochran, Buddy Holly, Gene Vincent, The Coasters, Jackie Wilson, Sam Cooke, Marvin Gaye, and *anything* Motown and Stax Records. Stax, of course, is where Cropper had been a part of making countless classic records. Without all these early American influences in music, there would have been no Rolling Stones, no Hollies, no Eric Clapton, no Led Zepplin, no Traffic, no Spencer Davis Group, and many others. Even the Beatles had six cover songs by US artists on their first album. Certainly, there would have been no Dave Mason. So, to have the time with someone like Steve Cropper and be on the same stage with someone I'd listened to and admired during my formative musical years was not just a career highlight, it was a life highlight.

After years of living in California, which is certainly one of the most beautiful states, it made more financial sense to move. I chose Northern Nevada. It's also scenic and picturesque, but even more attractive because I had a number of good friends who lived there. In 2014, I sold my home in Ojai, and Winifred and I moved to Northern Nevada, to another stunning valley, just on the outer slopes of Lake Tahoe in the Carson Valley.

A year later, I got a surprise call from Bruce Cohen, who had been managing The Doobie Brothers for years and owned a winery in Napa called BRC Cohen. Bruce put on an annual event at his winery that was hugely successful. The Doobies were the main act, and other acts included Huey Lewis and the News, Kenny Loggins, Eddie Money, Bad Company, Pablo Cruise, and others. I played a few of the festivals, so I got to know Bruce. He called to let me know The Doobies were going out with Journey. "Call John Barrick and see if you can get on this. Your name is in the hat." I finally was back on a tour, playing to 15,000 to 20,000 people a night. It was a successful tour, not only musically, but also socially. John McFee, Pat Simmons, and John Cowan from The Doobies, as well as Ross Valory and Neal Shon from Journey, would come out to sit in on my opening set. From the audience point of view, I think it was something special to see these artists come together.

Shortly after that tour, Pat Simmons, who had a home on Maui and had been performing at an annual New Year's Eve event to benefit the Maui Food Bank, said to me, "You should really come and do this. Let me talk to Shep." Shep Gordon, who manages Alice Cooper, has put on this event for several years. Winifred, of course, was all for this one. She had history with the islands, not only because of the gallery she owned but also because she had attended her freshman year of college at The University of Hawaii.

The event prior to the New Year's show was always held at Shep's house on the beach. Shep's guest list spans the globe, and he is just a great guy and host. Any musical guest who attends is invited to join in, but what really made this event at his house great for me was the casual setup that the musicians had. Mick would be on drums, Steven Tyler jumped in on a blues tune with me, and Michael McDonald, Pat Simmons, and even Jim Carrey leaped up on a song. The guests were interesting, the food was delicious, and the setting was awesome.

While I thoroughly enjoyed all the guests and artists in attendance, the one that glued this whole thing together was Willie K—a legend in his own right who is often referred to as the Hawaiian Jimi Hendrix, if ever there's an echo from the past. He was one of the most talented artists I've ever played with. We became friends, but sadly he passed away in 2020. I miss him, and I'm not alone in this: All of the 808 does as well.

We were on Maui for a week. Winifred thought it would be a great idea to look at some properties on the island. I had no intention of buying anything at the time, but we finished up finding a house in Wailea. We had the best of both worlds: a mountain house in the Sierras and one in one of the most beautiful places in the world, Maui. When the pandemic hit, we let our Nevada house go and moved things out to Hawaii. I was really happy we had our little place in the islands. Life is about choices, and, as it turned out, Winifred led us into one of the great ones.

Prior to the pandemic, I'd been telling Winifred (and the universe) that I really needed to take at least a year off. Things were catching up with me, health-wise—a thought that occurred to me in no uncertain terms when I caught my reflection in a full-length mirror. It was haunting. I was overweight and eating like shit. I could barely walk due to the pain in my left hip. Nearly sixty years of nonstop touring had blatantly and thoroughly taken their toll. I had the same internal shift I experienced when I decided to cut the cocaine from my daily routine. I needed to regain my vitality if I was ever going to tour again, let alone be there for Winifred.

Be careful what you ask for because the universe will supply it—and not always in the way one expects.

Winifred and I were in lockdown, like the rest of the world. Since I was brought up as an only child, it's not hard for me to amuse myself. I had a studio at home, but what to do? I'd just finished *Alone Together Again,* an entire re-recording of my first album *Alone Together,* which I was promoting on our tour. But now that tour had been cut short by the pandemic. Artists were doing performances via the internet, and I was being asked to do something to stay in touch with the fans. Live shows had been such a big part of my life. I was interested to see if I could translate a live performance online. I love a challenge, and I thrive on learning. This thought consumed my lockdown time. Music has always pulled me through dark moments.

I wanted it to be something special. John McFee sent me a video of The Doobies doing "Black Water." I was so impressed, and he turned me onto the videographer Rob Arthur (a great musician, too, who plays keys for Peter Frampton), who had put it together with all the artists being at home, in their own locations, recording it. This set me to thinking about inviting some artists to do "Feelin' Alright?" with me. Mick Fleetwood agreed, as did Michael McDonald, Sammy Hagar, Pat Simmons and his son Pat Simmons Jr., John McFee, Tom Johnston, John Cowan (bass player with the Doobies), and my drummer Alvino Bennett. I named this ensemble Dave Mason and the Quarantines as a bow to the shared experience all the world was all going through together. Our video can be viewed on our YouTube channel, which is @davemasontv.

Along with what we were doing professionally, it was due time—no, long overdue—to seriously take care of physical issues in my personal life. I dropped forty pounds, which helped some of the pain I was experiencing in my hip. But that was something that I could no longer put off. Even though we were in the throes of the pandemic, I chose to have my hip replacement surgery done at Stanford, which took place about a week before my seventy-fifth birthday. We'd recently met a new friend, a gentleman named Steve Cohen, who just bought a house in Makena in Maui. His business was on the mainland, in New York, one of the largest above-ground pool companies, and he generously offered to fly us to Santa Barbara on his company plane. Winifred was right there with me through the whole thing, thank God, as what we thought would be a few weeks before we flew back to Maui turned into a six-week stay. Thanks to a dear friend I've known since my days in Chicago, Steve Edelson, and his wife Angie, we got to convalesce in our former hometown of Ojai. Don't let anyone tell you that a full hip replacement isn't painful. That first two weeks after surgery would have been impossible for me to get through without Winifred. That beautiful setting we were in, and the kindness of the Edelsons, set me on the path of recovery. And as a lucky bonus, our return trip to the islands coincided with Mr. Cohen flying back to Maui, so we got a round trip!

Back on Maui, I resumed plans to promote *Alone Together Again,* including a vinyl edition, which had to be just as captivating as the original packaging with its three-panel fold out and specialty colored vinyl. Most of the songs are true to the original, with the exception of "World in Changes," which is completely different and perhaps appropriate to the times given the dramatic shifts taking place. I often play with new arrangements of songs, but most don't make it out to the public. In any event, for this version of "World in Changes," I chose to do a reggae version of it, for which I made a video out in the lava fields of south Maui. This led to two bands doing versions and remixes of it.

As we waited to start touring again, I kept my chops up by playing guitar on my couch, my patio, and in my makeshift studio where I wrote a handful of songs. The rest must have done me some good, not only physically but also mentally, as writing began to be fun and inspired again. I also did some live shows with Mick Fleetwood and his Island Rumors band. Mick has always been so generous inviting me in, and I really enjoyed performing with people and for people again.

We took two full years off touring but, in January 2022, I started back again and have been at it ever since. Touring these days is different and not necessarily as easy as it once was. But, as always, the music and the fans pull me through, as does a sense of amazement that I've made it this far. Not just living through a pandemic, mind you, but through all this abundant, unpredictable, not necessarily linear life. I do recognize my connection to music is what tethers me to this world, and I keep moving forward because that's all I really know how to do.

Pretty much 90 percent of what I do is a craft. It's my passion and drive to conjure the art into a finished piece of music. You can't see it and you can't touch it, but it's going to touch someone somewhere. The drive to master my craft keeps me moving forward. What I do is also how I make a living. Creating and recording new material, like anything, costs money. When radio was the way you heard new songs by an artist, the average royalty was between three and five cents per play. There was a time when 300,000 plays would earn an artist between $9,000 and $15,000. In sharp contrast, 300,000 to 350,000 streams (i.e., plays on Spotify, Pandora or Apple) will earn a songwriter roughly $1,000. Between the cost of making a record and the fact that there is no real way to get new music heard en masse, it becomes less and less economically feasible to sustain apart from playing live shows. Samual Clemens, better known as Mark Twain, personally lobbied Congress on behalf of writers to protect their intellectual property. The Internet, though a remarkable tool, has largely destroyed that.

And yet, I still make music. Of course I do. I can't imagine a life otherwise. What does the future hold? Maybe I'll be out there on the road literally until the end (don't miss the last show). The way this crazy life unfolds, I wouldn't be surprised if my biggest and best shows are ahead of me. One way or another, I'll be singing and playing guitar.

Don't It Make You Wonder

City girl's gonna make me crazy
Country boy in a brand new game
Never knew how they could change me
Almost make you want to go insane

Oooh it will make you wonder
Oooh it's a crying shame
Oooh it will drag you under
And you'll never be the same

Spend today what you make tomorrow
Ridin' high as your life goes by
Love is free and you pay for sorrow
You think you're living but you're dead inside

Oooh it will make you wonder
Oooh it's a crying shame
Oooh it will drag you under
And you'll never be the same

Get to wonderin' why I came here
Get to wonderin' why I even stay
Gotta be a damn good reason
Gotta find me a better way

Oooh it will make you wonder
Oooh it's a crying shame
Oooh it will drag you under
And you'll never be the same

Don't It Make You Wonder

If I had a dollar for every person who asked me if there would be a Traffic reunion, I'd be a very wealthy man. But that's not the point, really. Hundreds of thousands of fans still love the music, me included. Not to mention legions of younger audiences who've discovered the music, many of whom weren't even born when we were jamming at the cottage. Yes, I'm still a fan, regardless of what has happened. A concert with the two original members was on a lot of people's bucket list, including mine.

Did I ever ask, you say? Many times, directly and indirectly. The story I heard was that Jim Capaldi, on his deathbed, made Winwood promise he'd never go out on the road as Traffic again. I didn't want to believe it.

But I heard it directly from the proverbial horse's mouth. Winifred and I attended Winwood's concert at Humphrey's by the Bay in San Diego in 2017. We met Steve backstage after the show. When he appeared arms outstretched, any tensions I may have felt about meeting melted away. After a warm, extended hug, we caught up like two old mates, cheerfully recalling shared memories. Steve wanted to smoke a cigar, so we all stepped outside onto the balcony overlooking San Diego Bay.

Not wanting to waste the moment, I made an appeal. What everyone always asks about.

"Steve, that crowd you had out there tonight was great, but we could make it larger by twenty-fold and make a lot of people happy. Let's bring Traffic back."

Steve looked up, and after a long pause said, "Well, you know …"

I said, "I know Capaldi elicited a promise from you that you'd never go out as Traffic. And you promised Capaldi."

And Steve answered, "I promised Capaldi."

What started as a rumor had been confirmed.

I said, "We can call it something else. 'Traffic Jam.' Not just us. We could invite people in along the way, special guests like, say, Dave Matthews, who inducted us into the Hall, to help carry the torch and keep the music alive. Expand the musical family in the name of Traffic."

A nearby security guard who had caught the conversation leaned in and said to Winwood, "I don't know much about much, but you should listen to this man." Winwood's son, also standing by, seemed intrigued by the idea. Steve stood there rocking back and forth, arms folded, gazing up at the open sky and seemed to be giving it some deep thought. He didn't say anything, but he didn't say no. We chatted a bit more. Then the conversation ended. Was he considering it? I may never know. Another warm hug, this time to say goodbye, and that was the last time I saw Steve.

I'll never really understand what Capaldi's motives were at the end. It's such a selfish request, in my mind, anyway. And equally bizarre to me is that Winwood said yes. Music is bigger than the sum of its parts. What I don't understand is how what started as the most innovative, generous, and inclusive group of creatives I've ever worked with could shrink the extraordinary mystery of music to fit into one neatly packaged box.

It's true that hearing the music from original members holds a magic on its own. Yet, as much as it's about people, it's about the music, if not more so. The moment we unleashed our songs into the world, we surrendered ownership in the more mystical interpretation of the word— and Traffic was all about the mystic.

To even write about this gave me many moments of pause. Is this OK to talk about? Do I dare bare my soul in such a vulnerable way?

Ultimately, I am choosing to include it because I don't want to go to my grave with a heart hardened by disappointment. I choose, rather, to want all of us to be feeling alright, no question mark in sight.

Acknowledgments

My life has been touched by many, and there is no way to mention everybody, though I know who you are, and I'll always hold the memories of so many, many faces I've been honored to know over the decades. I am grateful for you all.

If it wasn't for the following people, and for a wide variety of reasons, seen and unseen, this book would have never been written. First, to my wife, friend, and real-life partner, Winifred. A very sincere and deep thank you to Chris Epting, Scott B. Bomar, Mick Fleetwood, Sheryl and Alice Cooper, Steven Tyler, Graham Nash, Robyn Russell, Mike and Candy Finnigan, Steve and Angie Edelson, Star, John Leonard, Michelle Leonard, Carol Smith, Leigh Taylor Young, Mara, Bruce Botnick, Ron Nevison, Margie Peeples, Al Schmitt, Lucy, Danny and Leslie Zelisko, Jim Manera, David Doumeng, Paul and Coleen Doumeng, Richard and Katarina Doumeng, Laura Doumeng, Terry Cohen, Jack and Monique Kellman, Jason Cooper, Bonnie Bramlett, Chris and Maggie Stewart, Jim McNulty, Joan Hurley, Paul and Sandy Antonello, Shep and Katie Gordon, Paul Shaker, Lisa Chappel, Ted Knapp, Bernard Lachner, Malcolm and Kelley McDowell, John and Cathe Sambataro, Chris Curtis, Franz and Janet Weber, Kosta and Julie Arger, Carl and Kim Staub, Keith Dehnert, Pat and Chris Simmons, John and Marcy McFee, John Cowan, Sammy Hagar, Michael McDonald, Willie Kahaiali'i, Steve Winwood, every member of any Dave Mason band and crew (including my current band and crew: Johnne, Ray, Marty, Mark, Andy, Craig, and Chris), Katie Fox, Erin Dvorachek, Melissa Dragich, Michelle Hinz, Jeff and Holly

LaPointe, Craig Bettinson, Kim Marden, Nick Audino, John, Joan and Lisa Inganamort, Farshid and Sara Khosravi, Craig Smith, Jim and Rosie Farmer, John and Kitty Procaccini, Mike and Laura Jones, Anna Manuel, Craig Doolittle, John and Trang Lehr, Jim Forrester, Mark Ott, Michael Grasso, Bill Eure, Jackie Smaga, Nick and Susan Pritzker, Christine Jernigan, Chris Jensen, Michael Jensen, Henry Root, Rick Bartolf, Matt Linesch, Carrie Tanner, Alec Vidmar, Melanie Wicker, Gene Montesano, Barry Perlman, Wayne Forte, Charlie Brusco, Carl Stubner, and Zach Martin.

Permissions

Lyrics

Baby...Please
Words and Music by Dave Mason
Copyright © 1973 Indaba Enterprises
Copyright Renewed
All Rights Administered by Sony Music Publishing (US) LLC, 424
  Church Street, Suite 1200, Nashville, TN 37219
International Copyright Secured. All Rights Reserved
Reprinted by Permission of Hal Leonard LLC

Bird on the Wind
Words and Music by Dave Mason
Copyright © 1978 EMI Blackwood Music Inc. and Dave Mason Music
All Rights Administered by Sony Music Publishing (US) LLC, 424
  Church Street, Suite 1200, Nashville, TN 37219
International Copyright Secured   All Rights Reserved
Reprinted by Permission of Hal Leonard LLC

Blow by Blow
Words and Music by Mark Holden, Dave Mason, and John Cesario
Copyright © 1994 Universal Music - MGB Songs, Dream Dealers Music,
  BMG Gold Songs, Exploration Group LLC, 26 12 Music and John
  Cesario Publishing Designee
All Rights for Dream Dealers Music Administered by Universal Music -
  MGB Songs

Can't Stop Worrying, Can't Stop Loving

Cool Runnin'

Don't It Make You Wonder

Feelin' Alright

Full Circle and Then

Copyright © 2008 BMG Gold Songs, Exploration Group LLC, 26 12
   Music and John L. Sambataro Publishing Designee
All Rights for BMG Gold Songs, Exploration Group LLC and 26 12
   Music Administered by BMG Rights Management (US) LLC
All Rights Reserved. Used by Permission
Reprinted by Permission of Hal Leonard LLC

Give Me a Reason
Words and Music by Dave Mason
Copyright © 1975 EMI Blackwood Music Inc.
Copyright Renewed
All Rights Administered by Sony Music Publishing (US) LLC, 424
   Church Street, Suite 1200, Nashville, TN 37219
International Copyright Secured. All Rights Reserved
Reprinted by Permission of Hal Leonard LLC

Headkeeper
Words and Music by Dave Mason
Copyright © 1971 EMI Blackwood Music Inc.
Copyright Renewed
All Rights Administered by Sony Music Publishing (US) LLC, 424
   Church Street, Suite 1200, Nashville, TN 37219
International Copyright Secured. All Rights Reserved
Reprinted by Permission of Hal Leonard LLC

Hole in My Shoe
Words and Music by Dave Mason
Copyright © 1967 UNIVERSAL / ISLAND MUSIC LTD.
Copyright Renewed
All Rights Administered by UNIVERSAL – SONGS OF POLYGRAM
   INTERNATIONAL, INC.
All Rights Reserved. Used by Permission
Reprinted by Permission of Hal Leonard LLC

Just a Song
Words and Music by Dave Mason
Copyright © 1970 EMI Blackwood Music Inc.
Copyright Renewed

Let It Go, Let It Flow

The Lonely One

Maybe

Mystic Traveler

Namaste
Words and Music by Dave Mason

Only You Know and I Know
Words and Music by Dave Mason

Road Dogs
    Words and Music by Dave Mason

Searchin' (For a Feeling)
Words and Music by Dave Mason

Shouldn't Have Took More Than You Gave
Words and Music by Dave Mason

Show Me Some Affection

Takin' the Time to Find

Two Hearts

Waitin' on You

Reprinted by Permission of Hal Leonard LLC

World in Changes
Words and Music by Dave Mason
Copyright © 1969 UNIVERSAL/ISLAND MUSIC LTD.
Copyright Renewed
All Rights in the United States Administered by UNIVERSAL - SONGS
    OF POLYGRAM INTERNATIONAL, INC.
All Rights Reserved. Used by Permission
Reprinted by Permission of Hal Leonard LLC

You Can All Join In
By Dave Mason
Copyright © 1968 UNIVERSAL/ISLAND MUSIC LTD.
Copyright Renewed
All Rights in the United States Administered by UNIVERSAL - SONGS
    OF POLYGRAM INTERNATIONAL, INC.
All Rights Reserved. Used by Permission
Reprinted by Permission of Hal Leonard LLC

Photographs

All images are from the collection of the author unless otherwise noted.

Photographs from text pages

Photos of Traffic on pages 3 and 44 © 1967 Paul McCartney / Photographer: Linda McCartney. All Rights Reserved.

Photo of Worcester Cathedral on page 5 by CaronB, and of New Street on page 6 by Johnnieb. Both via iStock by Getty Images.

Photo on page 31 courtesy of Jim Forrester.

Photos of Traffic rehearsing on pages 37 and 93 © Barrie Wentzell.

Photo of Mason with double neck acoustic on page 40, and playing electric guitar onstage on page 102 by Chris Walter / Michael Ochs Archives via Getty Images.

Photos of Traffic onstage on page 41, walking in Paris on page 61, and sitting on steps on page 201 from Pictorial Press Ltd / Alamy Stock Photo.

Photo of Mason with sitar on page 43 from ZUMA Press, Inc. / Alamy Stock Photo.

Photo of Winwood and Mason in the studio on page 48 by Brian Cooke / Redferns via Getty Images.

Photo of Mason with the Jimi Hendrix Experience on page 56 from the Michael Ochs Archives via Getty Images.

Photo of Mason and Joe Cocker on page 65 from the collection of Paul and Sandy Antonello.

Photo of Mason onstage with Cass Elliot on page 66 and of Mason with Ringo Starr's All-Starr Band on page 193 by Henry Diltz / Henry Diltz Photography.

Photos of Mason with guitar on page 67, performing with Delaney & Bonnie on pages 69 and 71, and backstage with George Harrison and Eric Clapton on page 72 are by Barry Feinstein / © Barry Feinstein Photography, Inc..

Photo of Mason and Eric Clapton backstage on page 77 by Koh Hasebe/ Shinko Music from the Hulton Archive via Getty Images.

Photo of Bonnie Bramlett on page 78 by Harvey Silver / Corbis Historical via Getty Images.

Photo of Mason in hat on page 83 by Eric Bachmann / © Eric Bachmann estate.

Photo of Bruce Botnick on page 86 by Scott Dudelson.

Photo of Masson with Cass Elliot and Ned Doheny on page 89 by Clive Arrowsmith / Camera Press.

Photo of Mason with the Pointer Sisters on page 99 © Photo by Dan Cuny

Photo of Mason with band on page 99 by Herb Greene.

Photo of Mason in the studio with Denny Laine and Paul McCartney on page 112 by Mario Algaze / Courtesy of the Mario Algaze Estate and PDNB Gallery.

Photo of Mason and band onstage on page 127 by Dick Barnatt / Redferns via Getty Images.

Photos of airplane and Margie Peeples on page 130 courtesy of Margie Peeples.

Photos of Russian concert crowd on page 182 and Mark Ott on page 184 courtesy of Mark Ott.

Photo of Mick Fleetwood on page 190 courtesy of Mick Fleetwood.

Photo of Traffic with their instruments on page 199 by Keystone Features / Hulton Archive via Getty Images.

Photo of Traffic with Mason in hat on page 200 from the GAB Archive / Redferns via Getty Images.

Photo of Mason speaking at the Rock & Roll Hall of Fame induction on page 202 by Kevin Kane / WireImage via Getty Images.

Photo of Mason performing at the Rock & Roll Hall of Fame ceremony on page 203 by KMazur / Wire Image via Getty Images.

Photo of Winifred Mason on page 212, Dave (in ball cap) and Winifred on page 216, Dave with guitar on page 219, and Dave and Winifred on final page by Chris Jensen.

Photo of Mason and Steve Cropper onstage on page 214 courtesy of Timothy Teague.

Photo of Willie K on page 215 courtesy of his estate.

Photographs from insert:

Photo of Traffic on insert page 3, and of Mason in white suite on insert page 13 by Michael Putland from the Hulton Archive via Getty Images.

Photo of Mason in yellow vest on insert page 3 and phot of Mason with band on insert page 12 from Pictorial Press Ltd / Alamy Stock Photo.

Photo of Traffic on insert page 4 by Keystone / Hulton Archive via Getty Images.

Photo of Mason in the studio on insert page 4 from the Estate of Keith Morris / Redferns via Getty Images.

Photo of Mason on insert page 5 and of Mason and Jimi Hendrix on insert page 6 are © 1967 Paul McCartney / Photographer: Linda McCartney. All Rights Reserved.

Photo of Mason onstage with Derek and the Dominoes on insert page 6 by Koh Hasebe/Shinko Music from the Hulton Archive via Getty Images.

Contact sheet on insert page 7 by Barry Feinstein / © Barry Feinstein Photography, Inc.

Photo of Mason with Cass Elliot and Ned Doheny on insert page 8 by Clive Arrowsmith / Camera Press.

Photo of Mason with band on insert page 8 by Herb Greene.

Photo of Mason in the studio with Wings on insert page 9 © 1975 Paul McCartney / Photographer: Linda McCartney. All Rights Reserved.

Upper left photo on insert page 10 © Alvan Meyerowitz/Retro Photo Archive.

Upper photo on insert page 14 by Dimitrios Kambouris. Lower photo by KMazur. Both from WireImage via Getty Images.

Photo of Winifred and Dave Mason on insert page 16 by Chris Jensen.

Thanks to the following for their assistance with photo clearances: Marcel Aeby, Clive Arrowsmith, Dominik Bachmann, Jay Blakesberg, Henry Diltz, Scott Dudelson, Missy Finger, Herb Greene, Jonathan Hyams,

Chris Jensen, Jake Jamison, Anthony McAndrew, Paul McCartney, Martha McClintock, Jordan Ohel, Rachél Ruderman, Gary Strobl, Timothy Teague, Barrie Wentzell, and Samantha Woodgate

Every reasonable effort has been made to seek permission to reproduce those images whose copyright does not reside with the author, and we are grateful to the companies and individuals who have assisted in this task. Any omissions are purely unintentional, and the details should be addressed to DTM Entertainment.

Dave Mason Discography

Official Solo Albums

Alone Together (1970)
Dave Mason & Cass Elliot (1971)
Dave Mason Is Alive (1972)
Headkeeper (1972)
It's Like You Never Left (1973)
The Best of Dave Mason (1974)
Dave Mason (1974)
Split Coconut (1975)
Certified Live (1976)
Let It Flow (1977)
Mariposo de Oro (1978)
The Very Best of Dave Mason (1979)
Old Crest on a New Wave (1980)
The Best of Dave Mason (1981)
Two Hearts (1987)
Some Assembly Required (1987)
Best of Long Lost Friend (1995)
Forty Thousand Headmen Tour (1999)
The Ultimate Collection (1999)
26 Letters–12 Notes (2008)
Future's Past (2014)
Traffic Jam (2016)
The Columbia Years: The Definitive Anthology (2016)

4 Real—Rock and Soul Revue Live with Dave Mason and Steve Cropper
    (2018)
Alone Together Again (2020)
A Shade of Blues (2024)

Other Solo Appearances

Somebody Help Me—Spencer Davis Group (1966)
Gimme Some Lovin'—Spencer David Group (1966)
I'm A Man—Spencer Davis Group (1967)
Scrapbook (1972)
The Very Best of Dave Mason (1974)
Skate Town USA (1979)
Live at Perkins Palace (1981)
Show Me Some Affection (1991)
Sounds of the 70's FM Rock 2 (1992)
Live at Sunrise (2002)

Fleetwood Mac Albums

Time (1995)
Soccer Rocks the Globe (1994)
Fleetwood Mac Family Album (1996)

Traffic

Dear. Mr. Fantasy (1967)
Traffic (1968)
Best of Traffic (1969)
Last Exit ((1969)
Welcome to the Canteen (1971)
Smiling Phases (1991)

Other Appearances

Electric Ladyland—Jimi Hendrix (1968)
Beggar's Banquet—Rolling Stones (1968)
Lily The Pink—Scaffold (1969)
Word of Mouth—Neil Merryweather (1969)
All Things Must Pass—George Harrison (1970)
Delaney & Bonnie and Friends on Tour with Eric Clapton (1970)
Motel Shot—Delaney & Bonnie (1971)
Songs for Beginners—Graham Nash (1971)
Winwood—Steve Winwood (1971)
Bobby Keys—Bobby Keys (1972)
Graham Nash and David Crosby (1972)
History of Eric Clapton (1972)
Wild Tales: Oh How We Danced—Jim Capaldi (1972)
Wild Tales—Graham Nash (1973)
Phoebe Snow—(1974)
Venus and Mars—Wings (1975)
Get Off II—Various artists (1975)
You Can't Argue with a Sick Mind—Joe Walsh (1976)
Thoroughfare Gap—Stephen Stills (1978)
Gimme Some Neck—Ron Wood (1979)
Airborne—Don Felder ((1983)
Classic Rock, Vol 1 (1988)
Crossroads—Eric Clapton (1988)
Best of Delaney & Bonne (1990)
Finer Things—Steve Winwood (1995)
After the Love—Various artists (1995)
All Day Thumbsucker Revisited—various artists (1995)
Time Life Music Guitar Rock—various artist (1971)

Dave Mason Biography

Dave Mason's career spans over half a century and encompasses producing, performing, and songwriting. Fans and critics alike hail Dave as one of the most talented songwriters and guitarists in the world—which is why he is still performing over 100 shows a year to sold-out crowds.

Mason has been playing guitar most of his life. By fifteen, Dave had founded two bands: The Deep Feeling and The Hellions. At eighteen, the Worcester, England, native teamed up with Steve Winwood, Jim Capaldi, and Chris Wood to form the legendary band Traffic. At twenty, Mason penned the song "Feelin' Alright?" The rock anthem, first recorded by Traffic and then covered by dozens of other artists (including Joe Cocker), cemented both Dave's and Traffic's legacy and had a profound influence over rock music that continues today.

Mason left Traffic in 1969 to pursue a solo career in the US. Dave has penned over 100 songs, has three gold albums—*Alone Together, Dave Mason*, and *Mariposa De Oro*—and a platinum album, *Let it Flow*, which contained the top-ten single "We Just Disagree."

In addition to cranking out hits, Dave has performed on or contributed to a number of famous albums, including The Rolling Stones' *Beggars Banquet*, George Harrison's *All Things Must Pass*, Paul McCartney and Wings's *Venus and Mars* and Jimi Hendrix's *Electric Ladyland*. Mason is featured playing acoustic guitar in "All Along the Watchtower" on *Electric Ladyland*, a favorite in Dave's live shows!

Dave, a prolific artist in his own right, has collaborated with an enviable list of the who's who in the music industry—Jimi Hendrix, George Harrison, Paul McCartney, Stevie Wonder, Michael Jackson,

Graham Nash, Stephen Stills, Rita Coolidge, Delaney & Bonnie, Leon Russell, Ron Wood, Steve Winwood, Eric Clapton, and Jim Capaldi, just to name a few. In addition to his own productions, Mason's distinctive work is featured on numerous Gold and Platinum albums such as:

- Jimi Hendrix, *Electric Ladyland,* "All Along The Watchtower" (acoustic guitar) and "Crosstown Traffic" (vocals)
- George Harrison, *All Thing Must Pass* (various tracks)
- The Rolling Stones, *Beggars Banquet,* "Street Fighting Man" (shehnai and mellotron)
- Paul McCartney and Wings, *Venus and Mars,* "Listen to What the Man Said" (guitar)
- Graham Nash, *Songs for Beginners*
- David Crosby & Graham Nash, *Graham Nash David Crosby*
- Dave Mason & Cass Elliot (Mamas & Papas), *Dave Mason & Cass Elliot*
- The Spencer Davis Group, "Somebody Help Me," "Gimme Some Lovin,'" and "I'm A Man" (vocals)
- Fleetwood Mac, *Time* (guitar, vocals)
- Eric Clapton, *Crossroads* (guitar)

When Dave is not touring, he spends his time writing and producing music in his home studio, as well as tirelessly supporting philanthropic efforts.